CW00422349

A Somerset Hero
Who Beat The Aussies

THE LIFE AND TIMES OF
J.C. "FARMER" WHITE

by Basil Ashton Tinkler

[signature]

WITH A FOREWORD BY MICHAEL HILL
President, Somerset C.C.C.

The Parrs Wood Press
MANCHESTER

First Published 2000

This book is copyright under the Berne Convention. All rights are reserved. Apart from any fair dealing for the purpose of private study, research, criticism or review, as permitted under the Copyright Act 1956, no part of this publication may be reproduced, stored in a retrieval system, or transmitted in any form or by any means electronic, electrical, chemical, mechanical, optical, photocopying, recording or otherwise without the prior permission of the copyright owner. Enquiries should be sent to the publisher at the undermentioned address.

THE PARRS WOOD PRESS
St Wilfrid's Enterprise Centre
Royce Road, Manchester, M15 5BJ

© Basil Ashton Tinkler

ISBN: 1 903158 05 2

This book was produced by Andrew Searle, Michael Clarke and Ruth Heritage of The Parrs Wood Press and Printed in Great Britain by:

Fretwell Print and Design
Healey Works
Goulbourne Street
Keighley
West Yorkshire BD21 1PZ

To Jan, who I love very dearly

CONTENTS

ACKNOWLEDGEMENTS

I am grateful to a number of people for answering my questions and supplying help, assistance and information in producing this book. The list of names is almost bound to exclude someone it should not, and any such person please accept my humble apologies. My thanks go to Tony Stedall and the Somerset Cricket Museum, Clifford Jiggens on how to bring a book to fruition, Tom White (J.C's son), Sara Knight (grand-daugher) for loan of the family album, Vic Robson for loan of his scrap-book, John Brown of Taunton School for loan of school magazines, Taunton and Bridgwater library staff, Mike Tarr, Hector Tuckfield, my wife Jan who was uncomplaining through the many hours I was closeted with my word processor, and elder son David, who read the first draft and declared it "a good read".

FOREWORD

JACK WHITE was my childhood hero, although I was too young to have seen him play. During the Second World War I was at school in the Quantock Hills. The library consisted mostly of history books belonging to my history master, one G.D. Martineau, an authority on cricket in the eighteenth and nineteenth centuries and a regular contributor to 'The Cricketer' for thirty years. My favourite book which I read and re-read was 'The Fight for the Ashes, 1928-29' by P.F. Warner when England, under the captaincy of A.P.F. Chapman, retained 'The Ashes' by four matches to one. That side was a strong one which included Hobbs and Sutcliffe, Hammond and Hendren, Larwood and Tate and Jack White. Wally Hammond, another of my heroes, scored 905 runs in that series at an average of 113 with four centuries, two of them double hundreds.

However, it was Jack White who caught my imagination most, being a Somerset man born and bred and a farmer (distinctions I share with him). He was a subtle, slow left arm bowler more notable for command of length and flight than for his powers of spin. It was this quality, added to his capacity to bowl economically for long periods, something he had acquired bowling on the batsman friendly pitches at Taunton, that brought about his shock selection at the age of thirty seven for his first major tour. This was attributed to Jack Hobbs, who had been co-opted as a selector. An inspired choice, White took more wickets (25) and bowled more overs (406) than any bowler on either side. His finest achievements came in the Fourth Test at Adelaide which England won by 12 runs on the seventh day (matches were played to a finish in that series). In 100 degree heat he took 5-130 in 60 overs in the first innings and 8-126 in 64.5 overs in the second.

Jack White is undoubtedly the finest slow bowler to play for

Somerset, taking over 2000 wickets for the county in his long career. In view of this, it is surprising that no-one before has attempted to write about him, other than in short essays by R.C. Robertson–Glasgow, E.W. Swanton and David Foot. Maybe it is because he was a dour, taciturn character who did not engender warmth in others. However I am sure all followers of Somerset cricket will be delighted that Basil Tinkler has filled this gap in the Club's history by writing this biography.

The author, a civil engineer by profession, has used his early years of retirement to research painstakingly the life and times of Jack White. This may be his first book, but I hope it will not be the last on Somerset players of the past. I commend it to all cricket lovers, particularly to those with Somerset connections.

Michael Hill
President, Somerset C.C.C.

1.

INTRODUCTION

IT WAS THE 9th February 1929 and a cold North wind blew across Lord's and, for that matter, the rest of England, but eleven thousand miles away in Adelaide the temperature had risen inexorably through the nineties, degree by degree, like a batsman intent on reaching the magic "ton". It was the fourth Test and England had already secured the Ashes, having won the first three Tests, but the English players were still performing as though their lives depended on it. The supreme prize of a clean-sweep against Australia, in Australia, in a Test series, was a real possibility.

This was the seventh day of a Test with no time-limit. Bradman had been run out, but not before he had helped the Australians to reach 326 for 8 wickets by lunch. Two wickets in hand and 23 runs required to win! The pitch was placid, and immaculately as White and Tate bowled, the runs gradually came until 13 were needed!

White searched in his trouser pocket for a sweat-soaked handkerchief and went through the charade of wiping his perspiring forehead and neck, the once white cloth was as wet as they were. He had called for a clean dry shirt more than once that day and had at intervals reinforced himself with the odd whisky and soda. He dried the sweat, which had run down his wrists on to his hands, on his trouser legs, steadied himself and with six measured strides, bowled again. Grimmett sensed it was short - you never quite knew against White - and went for the square-leg boundary, only to find that the ball had come on to him a little faster than he had expected, causing him to catch it high on the blade. Instead of the high arc to the boundary, as Grimmett had intended, the ball flew on a lower trajectory and thirty thousand Australian cheers were strangled at birth as Tate accepted the chance and plucked the ball out of the air in triumph.

The last man in was Blackie, who batted left-handed, and he negotiated the last four balls of the over. Tate bowled a maiden, his fifth in succession (one of the best spells he had ever bowled, he opined later) and

Oldfield could not rescue Blackie from having to face White again. The two teams, and indeed the whole crowd, seemed to know that if England were to win, it would be the sweat-soaked White who would achieve it. Even the ebullient Tate knew that he was playing a secondary role and was bowling for containment to let White get at Blackie again.

White started his 125th over of the match. Several times during this marathon Percy Chapman, the captain, had made his way over to have a word with Jack Hobbs, his senior professional. *"Shall I keep him on, do you think?"* Always he received the same answer. *"Let him keep going."* They both knew Jack White could bowl all day, and all night if needed. But 125 overs! Blackie played four balls safely and then he also saw one which looked a little shorter than the others and he could contain himself no longer. He laid back and hit. There was a quite audible, universal drawing in of the breath by the huge crowd, like an express train entering a tunnel. All eyes went skywards but, unfortunately for Blackie and all Australia, so did the ball. Larwood raced across from extra-cover to take the catch half-way to the boundary. England had won by 12 runs - after seven days!

Jack White had bowled 60 overs, 16 maidens, and taken 5 wickets for 130 runs in the first innings and followed that with 64.5 overs, 21 maidens, and taken 8 wickets for 126 runs in the second innings. On a wicket giving little help to the bowlers, it was a feat of sheer persistence and relentless accuracy over many hours in temperatures which would have made an iceberg boil.

Monty Noble, that great Australian captain of the beginning of the century, wrote:

"The one man who truly and actually won the Ashes was the capable, modest, unassuming and genial sportsman Jack White. He was the great rock and standby of his side and one of the most tireless workers with muscle and brain that this or any other English team of cricketers has ever possessed. His machine-like effort, unswerving purpose and dominating accuracy were accountable for so much timidity and indecision on the part of his opponents that he reduced them to a condititon of nervous tension and sapped their virility and courage to such an extent that few, if any, did themselves justice when opposed to his mentality and guile. He would keep plugging away with that slight variation of pace, flight, inswing and spin, so small in extent yet sufficiently deceptive to create just that element of apprehension which killed initiative and worried the opposition into defeat. It all looked so simple, yet how many men did he

gradually force back and back to their fatal discomfiture.

"Good, bad, or worn wickets alike, he was always able to call the tune and make the batsmen dance to it - and invariably the dance was that of death. There have been left-handers who had greater pace, swerve and break, but none possessed a better or more consistently good length, greater versatility and variation and made class batsmen scratch their way to doom."

Not a bad tribute from an Australian captain when talking about an Englishman!

When, some weeks later, the English party sailed home, they were feted as conquering heroes, which is of course what they were. In Somerset, Jack White received a royal welcome indeed; but that is something we must return to later because our story starts many years earlier. It is the story of J. C. (Farmer)White, who was to become arguably the best and most successful Somerset bowler of all time, and who was to be selected to play for England in 15 Test matches, often as vice-captain and on four occasions as captain. Great cricketers have said that White filled the gap as England's top slow left-hand bowler between the departure of Wilfred Rhodes and the arrival of Hedley Verity. There can't be greater praise than to be bracketed with those two phenomenons. It is also the story of the professionals and amateur players of Jack White's day, and these were the days when the professionals came out onto the field of play from one dressing room and the amateurs from another. Incredibly in those days between the wars, Jack Hobbs, the master batsman, would never think of addressing Jack White in any way other than as "Mr. White". In general, the amateurs respected the professionals. Cricket is a game of results and those results are only too available for all to see. The skills of the professionals were apparent from their scores and their batting averages and bowling analyses. The professionals "respected" their amateur colleagues in a rather different way, their livelihoods depended upon it, particularly when part of their pay depended on actually being chosen to play. It is perhaps inconceivable today that such a situation could exist without rancour, but it did. One might say that the Gentlemen were players, and equally all the Players were gentlemen.

2.

ZENITHS AND NADIRS

JACK WHITE was fortunate in his choice of parents as his father, T. L. White, was a keen if not too skilful cricketer himself, and in later years, when J.C. was away on tour, his father helped to supervise his son's farming business in his absence. His father came from across the Somerset/Devon County border in the village of Torweston, Sampford Brett; whilst his mother before marriage was a Miss Cornish of Hill Farm, Stogumber, Somerset. Hence the J.C. (Cornish) initial of J.C. White. T.L. White was a Parish, District, and later County Councillor. In recognition of his services to the community he was elected a County Alderman. He was also a magistrate and sat on the Williton Bench. He farmed first at Woodlands Farm, Holford, and then at Escott Farm, Stogumber(400 acres). He was a keen sportsman and always maintained a cricket field on his farm for the use of the village. In later years he was a regular at the County ground in Taunton to watch his eldest son J.C. playing for Somerset. R.C. Robertson-Glasgow, that most eloquent of cricket- writers and a more than useful "fast" man, observed that the father used to watch J.C. trundling away with his slow left-handers, *in a comfortable silence that was presumed to represent approval."*

In those days it was quite the thing for the landed gentry to host cricket matches on their land, when the cream of the local talent would be summoned to show their skills against an invited eleven, and one can imagine the care which would be lavished upon "the square" prior to such proceedings. Robertson-Glasgow recalls blotting his copybook at one such event held at the estate of Sir Dennis Boles at Bishops Lydeard, not a stone's throw from where J.C. was farming. Jack White was his captain on this occasion and the 18 year old Robertson-Glasgow was called up to bowl and asked whether the fielders were placed to his liking. Casting around he noticed the host standing by the sight-screen, in conversation with his butler. Without hesitation he called, *"Up a bit Boles!"* In those days when "position" was courteously (and perhaps fearfully) acknowledged, the abruptness and titular inaccuracy of this request caused many of the players to turn away and smother their laughter and those in the furthest distance to collapse in uncontrolled mirth. Jack MacBryan in later years on the County circuit, during a dull period of a match, was wont to turn to Robertson-Glasgow from mid-off as the latter prepared to bowl and whisper from the side of his mouth *"Up a bit Boles".*

Apparently, Burgess the butler was something of a humourist, and when the head of the family was not looking, he used to pretend to trip with a tray full of drinks. To complete Robertson-Glasgow's memories of Bishop's Lydeard, he tells how the church there used to be attended by one of the loudest singers he had ever heard. He was a butcher who had been removed from the choir after some unseemly dispute about his required share in an anthem. His revenge was to sit in the front pew and drown the choir. R-G having considerable power of lung was put up as a rival and reports that he at least had the satisfaction of making the voce forte butcher turn around and stare *"with rubicund and surly amazement".*

J.C. was the eldest of three brothers and was educated at Taunton School where he was a boarder from 1903 to 1907. The school had opened in 1847 with a Dr. Bewglass as headmaster and 74 boarders, and had expanded at a steady rate thereafter. As with most organisations, it had then had its sticky patch, until at the end of the nineteenth century Dr. Whittaker had arrived to take over as headmaster, and the school had benefited by his drive and flair and began to prosper once more, with some 300 pupils. J. C. was fortunate to arrive at the school as it flourished under the direction of Dr. Whittaker, who introduced a number of innovations into the running of the school. One such innovation was the engagement of a professional cricketer to help coach the boys and staff in a pursuit which was considered desirable for the development of the character as well as providing exercise and entertainment of an acceptable kind. This was an innovation of which Jack White took full advantage as we shall see later.

A whole grove of walnut trees had existed in the grounds of the school in the early years, but by the time of J.C.'s attendance, they had been reduced to one grand old tree, which stood just inside the boundary of the cricket field. This location was extremely inconvenient to batsmen as it frequently prevented potential six-hits from reaching the boundary. Paradoxically, it must have been a boon to the less competent bowlers. Its generous crop of walnuts made it popular and boys liked to climb it, though this was forbidden. Cricketers had a love-hate relationship with it and J.C. White was once beaten for climbing it after being expressly forbidden to do so. The tree lead a precarious life for many years with advocates for its removal being outmanoeuvred on a number of occasions by its supporters for its survival. Poems were written about it, and Old Tauntonians, recounting their schooldays, waxed lyrical about it. Eventually the inevitable happened and the tree had to make way for progress. The appointed day for its execution arrived in 1923 and the event was attended by the whole of the school, with prize-giving and general merriment - a real festival occasion. Sad really; but the sadness was relieved because the School had the good sense not to simply consign the old tree to the bonfire. The wood was stored away to reappear in different guises at appropriate times in the future. After J.C. 's successful tour of Australia in 1928/29, he was presented with a shield made from the wood of the old tree. A special event was organised for the presentation, and it is said that J.C. was overawed by the *"educational atmosphere"* of the event. However he rose to the occasion and his acceptance speech was received with acclaim. In the afternoon he captained an M.C.C. side against the School. White took 6 for 14 (did he have to) including the wicket of R.A. Gerrard, who was later to become a renowned Rugby international. The School was saved from the ignominy of defeat by the rain (and I expect the ghost of the old walnut tree).

Quoting from the School magazine of the time, *"On the morning of the M. C. C. game, the School assembled in the Covered Playground to witness the presentation of a suitably engraved Shield of College Walnut to Mr. J.C. White, to signify their appreciation of his doughty deeds in Australia. The Head introduced Mr. White with an enconium of eulogistic superlatives, and placed the proceedings on a high level. F. H. Stevens made the presentation, to the accompaniment of great applause. Mr. White, replying, seemed at first a trifle overawed by the educational atmosphere, and dealt in detail with points of interest on the voyage to Australia. Speaking of his experiences on the cricket field, he confessed to one lamentable lapse from grace when he played out time by adjusting his bootlace. He had with him some interesting mementoes, specimens of Adelaide wicket, which the school were privileged to inspect."* It is intriguing to wonder about those specimens. Whatever did the Adelaide groundsman think to seeing part of his pitch disappearing?

Did other cricketers make a habit of acquiring part of the pitch? The ball, yes; the bails, yes; the stumps even, yes; but the pitch! The only reasonable conclusion must be that White's bowling on that pitch had been so exceptional that an exceptional stance was taken in allowing him to have, or, indeed, presenting him with a specimen from the hallowed turf. There is one other explanation of course. After being beaten, the Aussies may have decided that they would dig up the pitch and start again!

Geoffrey Moorhouse's book "Lord's" includes an absorbing page on pitches and the soil content thereof. The Soil Science Unit at the University of Wales, encouraged by the M.C.C., conducted a series of tests on the English county cricket grounds around the country during 1966 and 1967 to determine the degree of bounce in the wickets and how it related to the clay content of the soil. A standard English cricket ball when dropped on to a concrete surface from a height of sixteen feet will bounce 52 inches. On a very fast cricket pitch, the comparative bounce is over 30 inches and on a slow pitch less than half of that height. The University people found that the highest bounce was 30 inches at Worcester, where there was a clay content of 42% in the soil and there was a regime of heavy rolling from early Spring to harden the wicket. At Lord's the clay content was 35% and the bounce was 19 inches. It is interesting how much faster and bouncier some of the Australian and Caribbean wickets are, and which is often simply attributed to their hotter climates. In fact, the clay content at Melbourne was 48% and the bounce of a cricket ball was 31 inches. At Adelaide and Sydney the clay content was 52% and the bounce at each was 33 inches; whilst Brisbane had a clay content of 73% and a bounce of 41 inches. Sabina Park at Kingston, Jamaica had figures of 49% clay and 32 inches.

These figures show not only how touring sides must adjust to the conditions in the host country, but also how County sides have to perform on wickets much different from their home pitch as they travel around the various counties. Of course there are many other factors which help to determine how a pitch will play on a particular day, not least the weather and the atmospheric conditions, but it can be seen that it can be in the best interests of particular types of players to do a little research first before they choose where to base themselves and therefore play the majority of their matches. A fast bowler for example, all other things being equal, should base himself where the clay content of the pitches is high and the club owns a good heavy roller with the will to use it. Fortunately all other things are seldom equal. In any case, most County players at the start of their careers are pleased to be taken on by somebody (or even anybody) without ever having the luxury of choice of venue. The type of pitch is, however, something which established overseas players when joining a County for a season should be taking into account, but I suspect that the financial terms of the contract take much higher priority! Incidentally, one of the main reasons for annual top-dressing on many "squares", is to maintain or improve the clay content of the soil. If left to its own devices the content of the soil might easily diminish through leaching and associated climatic factors.

It does appear to me that this subject of pitches, clay content of the soil etc., should receive much more consideration than currently appears the case. Why don't Counties make up their square with a range of pitches of different soil characteristics. When the visiting team is full of strapping West Indian quickies, they could use the pitch with low clay content, a featherbed wicket which would help to draw their barbs. After assessing the make-up of the next opposing team, they could use the wicket least likely to give them assistance. Indeed they could take it a stage further by having different soil one end of the pitch from the other. The home team would know which end to play their best fast-bowler etc. The visiting teams would have to learn the hard way. As it is quite possible to dig up a pitch at the end of the season, they could further baffle the opposition by a different mix of pitches the following year. It is agreed that nothing affects the outcome of a match more than the pitch, so why don't the possibilities of ensuring a home advantage receive more investigation. I suppose at one time that wouldn't have been considered "cricket", but today. . . .

To return to the progress of J.C. White through life, we find him in 1903 as a 12 year old commencing his secondary education as a boarder at Taunton school. His home was only six miles away, but transport at that time was laboured and, anyway, his father no doubt decided that he should benefit from a full public school education, including boarding. About his academic abilities we know only a little, but we do know that these existed because he regularly appeared in the list of recipients at the annual prize-giving. Many pupils aspire to either the Arts side of the curriculum or alternatively to Science. On the strength of the prizes he received, it is not possible to locate J.C. in one camp or the other. In the Lower Fourth, he received the Writing Prize and with it the College of Preceptor's certificate. The prize, whether by choice or simply allocated, is not known, was a copy of "Naturalist's Library." It seems most appropriate whoever chose it, and it does not need much imagination to assess that this son of a farmer, living in the beautiful countryside of West Somerset on the edge of the Quantock Hills, would have produced knowledgeable essays on farming and wildlife.

It is known that J.C. passed the Lower Forms examination, even if it is not quite known what that was! In 1906, whilst in the Upper Fourth, he received a form prize and the College of Preceptor's certificate. It is not known what he accomplished to warrant receipt of this prize, which was a copy of "The Fairy Queen", nor is it considered that there would be any great merit on debating the matter. Continuing with his academic successes, before we turn to cricket, we find him in the Fifth Form in 1907. Having decided on the strength of his previous prizes that we have an Arts graduate in the making, we are totally undone when we discover that the versatile J.C. has landed the Arithmetic Prize. Whether the headmaster of the day had a leaning towards the Arts, whether there was a mix-up, or whether there was an allocation of books of certain titles which had to be dispensed, it is not known, although I am rather inclined to favour the latter. The fact of the matter is that the prize for Arithmetic was a copy of "Macaulay's History of England". J.C. also gained his Cambridge Preliminary Certificate at this time. It seems that was the end of his academic leanings for he was withdrawn from the school later that year at the age of sixteen. Presumably his father considered that he had enough education to satisfy his requirements for the life of a farmer, a destiny of which there was probably never any doubt.

J.C. had cricket bred into his bones. It was not the only Summer pastime in the Vale of Taunton between the Quantocks and the Brendon Hills, but it was a social aspect of life which was enjoyed wholeheartedly by the folk of the farms and villages. Involvement in cricket at school would have been as natural to J.C. as midnight feasts and practical jokes. It has already been mentioned that one of Dr. Whittaker's innovations was the appointment of a professional cricketer to help with the coaching of boys and masters. At that time there was a number of different levels of cricket at the school. The masters supplemented by the best of the senior boys played regular matches. The senior boys played first and second XI matches and then there were junior matches. The professional appointed to coach was a regular Somerset County player, E.J. Tyler, though of course in those days of "us and them" he was plain Tyler, his initials not counting. Tyler was a member of the Somerset County side when it was admitted to the County Championship in 1891. It had performed well in previous years against County opposition and was admitted as the ninth County.

In its early championship career Somerset had mixed fortunes but was always capable of providing an upset against the best sides. In its first year, Tyler took 57 wickets at an average of 20.16. The inimitable Sammy Woods headed the Somerset bowling averages with 134 wickets at an average of 16.97. It is surprising to find that the great W.G. Grace was having a lean time with the bat and that season averaged less than twenty. Bowlers seem to have dominated, because J.B. Challen of Somerset was sixth in the national batting averages with only 26.4. In only their second year in the championship, Somerset finished third in the table. It would be 1958 before they repeated the feat. Like most teams, they had their high spots and their low spots. A batting high came in 1892 at Taunton when Lionel Palairet and Bert Hewett put on 346 for the first wicket against Yorkshire. At the time this was a world record and remained so for a further five years. To this day, it is a Somerset record for any wicket. Palairet and Hewett were both Oxford Blues - an early example of Somerset's dependence on Varsity amateurs. There was no happy ending to this particular story because Hewett, who was the Somerset captain at the time, resigned after disagreement over his tactics against the tourists that year and seldom played again. Tyler had one of his many good days in the Yorkshire match, taking seven wickets for 111 off 50 overs.

A batting low came in the following year when Somerset were the unfortunate victims of a stumping record. At Cheltenham, the Gloucestershire pair of W.H. Brain (wicket-keeper) and C.L. Townsend (bowler) combined to pull off a hat-trick of stumpings. This was and still is unique in the annals of first-class cricket. The feat is all the more remakable when one studies the two performers. Brain had just come down from Oxford where he won a blue for cricket in each of his three years, and also a blue at soccer as a goalkeeper. It was the only season that he played County cricket. Townsend was still a Clifton schoolboy at the time and it was his second game for Gloucestershire! He was a leg-spinner and went on to have a very successful career as an all- rounder. The third victim in the hat-trick was none other than E.J. Tyler. In spite of the hat-trick Somerset comfortably won the match.

In 1895, Edwin Tyler had perhaps his greatest day when he disposed of the entire Surrey team, taking all ten wickets for 49 runs. The only Somerset player to emulate that feat is his protege - J.C. White.

In 1895 Somerset were on the receiving end when A.C. MacLaren, the Lancashire and Old Harrovian batsman, broke the great W.G. Grace's record for an individual innings in a first class match, which had stood at 344 for nineteen years. MacLaren scored 424 after batting for a day and a half. 93 years later, Graeme Hick of Worcestershire also exceeded 400 runs in his innings at Taunton. The Lancashire total of 801 was also a record, as the highest innings in County cricket. Apparently this total had twice been exceeded in first class cricket, one of which was the 803 scored by the Non-Smokers against the Smokers in 1887 on the East Melbourne ground in Australia. Scope there for the anti-smoking lobby's advertising, one would have thought. At the time of the Lancashire game, declarations in the first innings were not allowed, so unless batsmen were prepared to throw away their wickets, friendly pitches could realise very large totals. The rule to prevent a first innings declaration was presumably a throwback to the days when heavy gambling took place and was one of the measures to combat manipulation of the result. Incidentally, the Lancashire score was achieved in eight hours, so a rate of 100 per hour throughout suggests some entertaining watching. Unfortunately the majority of watchers were Somerset folk not Lancastrians.

In 1898, at Lord Hawke's instigation, a meeting was convened of County representatives to debate future arrangements for matches in this country between England and Australia. The main resolution carried was that the M.C.C should appoint a Board to govern such future Test matches. It was then resolved that the Board should comprise the President of M.C.C. and five of its club committee, and a representative from each of six counties, selected by the M.C.C. This may appear heavily biased towards the M.C.C., which of course it was. But it was the first erosion of M.C.C. powers, and it was to take almost the whole of another century before that august body was to be deprived of its dominant position in the world of cricket.

In 1899 Somerset had the ignominy of being beaten in 3 hours 5 minutes play by Middlesex at Lord's, scoring 35 and 44. Conditions must have been somewhat suspect on that day as Middlesex could only manage 86 in their innings. I wonder what today's T.C.C.B. pitch inspector would have made of it. Perhaps my earlier comments on "tailored" wickets isn't a new idea.

In 1900 the six-ball over was legalised. In England, when the first Laws were established in 1744 by "the London Club", an organisation about which little else is known, there were four balls to the over. This was the official position until 1889 when the five-ball over was introduced.

Incidentally, the Australians had played six-ball overs for some time, and later in 1918 were to change to eight-ball overs.

1900 also saw the introduction of the optional follow-on. Until that time it had been mandatory to impose the follow-on. It is known that there had sometimes been some strange bowling towards the end of an innings if the captain who would have to request the follow-on did not fancy final use of the wicket and was not therefore desirous of requiring the opposition to bat for a second time immediately. Another innovation around the time of the start of Tyler's career concerned the bowling. Until 1889 a bowler was permitted to change ends only once in an innings. The change which is still in force today allows him to change ends whenever his captain wishes, always providing that no bowler can bowl two overs consecutively, and all the balls in any one over must be bowled from the same end.

Before being employed to coach by Taunton School, Tyler had coached at Winchester College. Indeed, he was not very popular with certain members of the Somerset County administration for this, as they thought that it interfered with his County cricket. There was one example when he injured a leg whilst coaching at Winchester and reported on the eve of Somerset's game against Middlesex at Lord's that he might be unfit to play. It is reported that Somerset's amateur captain had a face as black as thunder at the prospect of being deprived of his star bowler, and when Tyler did appear and declare himself fit to play, *"the clouds rolled away and a beneficent smile was bestowed on all."* Nevertheless, there were those who thought that Tyler should devote himself to one master rather than try to serve two. Presumably his move to Taunton School at least had the advantage of locating him within the County so that an eye could be kept on him.

As the new century dawned Somerset continued to upset the best counties, and in 1901 it was Yorkshire's turn to suffer. This was to be Yorkshire's only defeat in 27 championship matches and they were fielding a full team at Headingley. All seemed to be going well for the Tykes, indeed very well. Somerset had been dismissed for 87 in their first innings and Yorkshire had replied with 325. L.C.H. Palairet and Braund, the Somerset openers, had both been dismissed for ducks in the first innings. Second time around, they took a fearful revenge and had 200 on the board in two hours. The Yorkshire bowlers never recovered and Somerset went on to total 630 (a County record at the time) in less than seven hours! The championship leaders' batsmen proved to be as overwhelmed as their bowling colleagues had been and the side was all out for 113, leaving Somerset the victors by 279. One of Sammy Woods' many stories arises from the event. Apparently, he and several others of the Somerset team had dined with the mayor of Leeds on the night before Somerset's second innings, and the mayor, presumably a canny Yorkshireman, knowing the state of the match, had promised £100 for the Somerset funds if they won. The £100 was never received, but Sammy was not too upset as he claims to have had a bet at 10 to 1 that Palairet would get a hundred in his second innings after failing in the first with a duck, and Palairet did the business.

In 1906 Yorkshire had their revenge - in a big way. The famous pair of Hirst and Rhodes had one of their glory days. Hirst had made 111 in the first innings and Yorkshire had a lead on first innings of 243. They elected not to enforce the follow-on, and Hirst and Rhodes scored 202 in 75 minutes without being separated. Hirst scored his second century of the match, in 66 minutes. Rhodes took half-an-hour longer. Hirst had bowling figures of 11 for 115 and Rhodes mopped up most of the others. Not surprising that they still talk in awe about George Hirst and Wilfred Rhodes in Yorkshire.

As a left-arm slow bowler we shall be giving more consideration to Rhodes, particularly in comparison with J.C. White and others of that ilk; but it is proper here to briefly pay homage to Hirst, who was a cricketer of few equals.

George Hirst (1871-1954) batted right-hand and bowled left-hand and was the greatest all-rounder of his day and 1906 was his best of many good years. Strangely, although he played in 24 tests he was unable to reproduce his County achievements. He was a nippy swing bowler and an aggressive batter. In 1906 he scored 2385 runs and took 208 wickets! This is the only occasion that the double of 2000 runs and 200 wickets has been achieved in a season. He is also the only man to score centuries in each innings and to take five wickets in each of the opponent's innings. He achieved the double of 1000 runs and 100 wickets on no less than 14 occasions, eleven of them in consecutive years; and I haven't finished yet. In 1906, he reached his "double" in just 16 matches, before the end of June! Some player, George Hirst!

As if the Yorkshire match wasn't bad enough, Somerset were to face an even tougher day the next year at Lord's. The occasion was Albert Trott of Middlesex benefit match. He was an Australian - the idea of importing them to bolster a County side is nothing new. As we all know, such matches are frequently a playing nightmare for the beneficiary, presumably because of the importance of the occasion and his great desire to put on a bit of a show. These extra pressures can result in something of a let-down. Well, it seemed that it might be going that way for Albert. He had not done anything to write home about, until the second wicket fell in Somerset's second innings. On being called upon to bowl, he proceeded to have Lewis l.b.w. , next ball he bowled Poyntz, next ball he bowled Woods, and lo and behold, next ball he bowled Robson. Four wickets in four balls! The next ball shaved the wicket and so convinced was the wicket-keeper that it had accounted for the new batsman that he let it go for four byes. But wait, Albert Trott had only just started. A few runs were scored, and then Trott wove his magic once more. Mordaunt was caught off his fourth ball of the over, Wickham was bowled next ball, and Bailey the last man had only one ball to face to see the over out. It was Bailey who was out. Trott had achieved his second hat-trick within half-an-hour of the first.

The match report states that the light was very poor, but that was not the major contributory factor to the batsmen's downfall. Well flighted bowling and the uncomfortable necessity of batting under unpleasantly dramatic conditions were the causes of the collapse. Trott's success had a touch of irony, as the match was over by lunch-time. Had it proceeded into the afternoon, it is thought that there would have been a large attendance, and Trott would have benefited financially. One Somerset player came out of the debacle with credit, and that was Braund the opening batsman who carried his bat right through the innings. The Times newspaper was quite perky with itself, because only the day before it had commented on how reliant Somerset were on one or two batsmen and here was the proof, amply demonstrated. Whether the financial loss from the early-finishing match was the principal cause of Albert Trott's succeeding penury will never be known, but within four short years he had suffered mental illnesses and finally shot himself at the age of only 41.

Whilst these zeniths and nadirs in Somerset C.C.C.'s fortunes were occuring, J.C. White was proceeding through the various levels of education - academic and cricket - at Taunton School. It was a fortunate turn of fate that Tyler should arrive at the school just after J.C., and there is little doubt that this coincidence was the crucial factor which launched J.C. on his successful career as one of the nation's best left-arm slow bowlers of all time.

It is variously reported that his mentor was E.J. Tyler of Somerset renown or, alternatively, a Mr. Newport, the Taunton school cricketing master who also turned out on occasions for the County. The official school history suggests that it was the latter who had the honour, but sentiment leans heavily towards the former. After all, Tyler was a slow left-arm bowler and one of considerable merit. Before the turn of the century Tyler was known to give the great W.G. himself some heartaches in the annual Somerset v. Gloucestershire battles. J.C., himself, shares the honour between them. Mr. Newport gave him great encouragement and stopped him from bowling too fast - a schoolboy fault if ever there was - when he joined the school, but it was Tyler who taught him the basics and then the subtleties of slow left-arm bowling. How much more satisfactory it must be for the tutor to be able to demonstrate to his pupil what is required and how to do it than to have to rely on simply talking about it.

At the beginning of the century, The Taunton School magazine, "The Tauntonian", used to report in some detail on the cricket matches in which the school were involved, and therefore there is a very full record of J.C.'s progress. It is interesting that the Whites had an involvement with Taunton School cricket before J.C. was old enough to play. Tom White (the father) was the patron of Stogumber village cricket, and their annual calendar of fixtures included home and away matches against Taunton School. It was the Boys' first XI which used to play in these matches, and the away fixture for the School was always one of their favourite matches, irrespective of the result, because Mrs. White traditonally laid on the catering. This might be tea or it might be luncheon, or it might be both; but whichever it was, it was always a splendid and lavish affair, which made the boys' eyes boggle. It was of such a standard and quality (and I imagine quantity) that it merited a mention each year in the match report, and sometimes even ascended to inclusion in the School magazine notes on the cricket highlights of the year. The level of achievement is perhaps best illustrated by the fact that no other catering was ever mentioned in the cricket notes.

In the 1905 matches against Stogumber, the School had a good win at home, and then travelled to Stogumber for the luncheon. . . sorry, return match. Tom White had not applied the roller with quite the same dedication with which he normally attended to all cricketing matters. The school magazine described the pitch as *"very fiery and treacherous"*. If the idea was to give the home side an advantage, perhaps thinking that the country swains would deal less fearfully with a rearing ball than the young public schoolboys, it badly misfired for Stogumber were all out for 94, of which Tom White scored 24. The school made 142 for 6.

Searching for information about that period of Jack White's career, I made a visit to Stogumber one Saturday afternoon, when I knew the team were playing at home. I was delighted to find the new cricket field, not too far removed from that of the White era, in as pristine a condition as a County ground. It boasted a slope like Lord's, though one would have to admit "slightly" more so. A neat little pavilion stood at the head of the field, looking down on the play, and laid out inside was a delightful tea, prepared by a lady who obviously enjoyed the duty. Mr. and Mrs. Tom White would have been very proud to see that Stogumber was maintaining its standards. I won't tell you the score on that particular afternoon, it wouldn't help the image.

Unfortunately nobody could point me in the direction of any old records of days gone by. The best they could do was to direct me to the home of Hector Tuckfield, one-time stalwart of the team, but now finding advancing years made even getting to the ground to watch too much effort. Hector could shed no light on where past records might lie, but he did remember Jack White and the fact that he was good with the boys in the village. He recalled that the students from Hartnoll Manor played for the village team and J.C., in the nets, would place a half-crown on the middle stump for anyone who could hit it.

Quite rightly Stogumber is more concerned with the present than the past, but don't get the impression that they have forgotten all about their heritage. The village pub boasts old photographs of cricket teams of yore and they are liberally sprinkled with Whites.

The 1906 School cricket notes pick out C.L. Lewis as the star bowler and he received the cricket bat for the best bowler at prize-giving day. Study of the individual matches support that award, as his haul of wickets was large and seldom did he fail to turn in an impressive bowling analysis. *"Lewis had most of the work to do, and did it excellently; he developed a fine pace, which, combined with a striking delivery, did wonders. He tired rather soon as might be expected, but usually after the damage had been done ... J. White and A. Ferrier did most of the work left - White has a good delivery, and a deceptive swerve sometimes. With a better pitch* (White's, I think, not the School's)*, and a little more head, he should be very useful next season."* The writer of these observations would be well pleased in later years, because of all his assets as a bowler, J.C. became famous for his unerring length and the thought with which he bowled.

For any supposed batsmen undergoing a long dry spell (of runs), the cricket notes provide an excuse which might have escaped them. *"Collier is essentially a slow wicket batsman, and seemed unable to appreciate the dry summer."*

Although only in the Upper Fourth form in 1906, J.C. played several times in the Masters/Boys team and took seven wickets for 162 runs at an average of 23.14 (the magazine states 27.00, so obviously the cricket master was not the maths master). For the Boys' First XI, J.C. took 29 wickets at the very commendable average of 14.72. W.L. Lewis, the quick bowler, took 43 wickets at 9.23. He deserved the prize bat, but somehow it doesn't seem right that a star bowler should receive a bat as the prize. I suppose bats are personal possessions which cricket balls are not. J.C. scored 109 runs at an average of 15.87.

I like to think that there was a degree of rivalry between White and Lewis, but Lewis was a year older and a form higher and that makes a big difference at the ages of 15 and 16, so perhaps White looked up to the older boy with the target of emulating him. Be that as it may, in the School House matches, White certainly came out on top when their respective houses played each other. White made 41 before Lewis bowled him, whilst White bowled Lewis for 0 and 4.

If Jack White was a promising cricketer in 1906, the following year saw him replace Lewis (now in the list of Valete) as the star man. On prize-giving day he received no less than three cricket bats. The first was for the best batting average, 28.3, for the combined Masters/Boys team i.e. the premier team of the school. The second was for the best bowling average - an amazing 6.1. This was for the Boys First XI. Unfortunately, the total of wickets is not given in the magazine, but reference to the individual matches suggests it would not be a long way short of a hundred wickets. The third bat was presented to him for his outstanding batting, which included scores of 64 not out, 57 not out, and 55. Edwin Tyler's tuition was bearing fruit.

The cricket notes for the season read, *"J. White was the cricketer of the team. At the commencement of the season he was a valuable batsman though somewhat cramped in style. His bowling was good always, and at the close it had become unplayable. His fielding was good, and he brought off some very smart slip catches. He thoroughly deserved his trial with Somerset Colts, and will we hope soon figure in the County team."* J.C. had become a prolific all-rounder, and in the matches against Stogumber he took many wickets, top-scored in one match, and had his father caught for one just before the close. An early example of the fact that he always played to win, whatever the circumstances - but always fairly. The luncheon and tea provided by Mrs. White at Stogumber were of the usual five-star standard and were acknowledged as such in the School magazine.

Some delightful pen pictures from the cricket notes will be recognisable to those who have fearfully awaited their school reports at the end of term:

W. A. Bell showed little improvement on last year's form.

O. W. Berry did not turn out the bowler we had hoped. He lost his pitch without which slow bowling is innocent.

J. B. Hill when keeping wicket appeared well padded; he prefers slow bowling. (That wasn't going to impress his father greatly - what a cruel thing to write for all to see!)

A highlight of the School season was the match at home against Bridgwater, when Sammy Woods turned out for the visitors. It was much appreciated and caused a major increase in the number of spectators, cameras and autograph books being prominent.

The School magazine again acknowledged the contribution made by E.J. Tyler, to give him his full title, and particularly commented on his untiring energy and geniality. He wouldn't know then, or perhaps he would, that he had launched one of England's great cricketers on his way.

3.

BEFORE THE WAR

IN 1909 JACK WHITE was chosen for his first County game, and thus he entered the stage of wondrous Somerset legends, some passed, some still playing, and others yet to arrive. By the time he departed that stage nearly thirty years later, he had earned for himself a place near the middle of the front row. We would need another book to deal with these legends in even a cursory manner, so all we can hope to do here is to meet those who Jack White met as he progressed through his life as an amateur cricketer.

Sammy Woods, that engaging character who everyone seemed to love, who had played for both Australia and England, and who led Somerset for thirteen seasons, had just hung up his bat and boots, though he was to play a very active part off the field for many more seasons. John Daniell was captain, and he was to emulate his predecessor Woods by captaining the side for thirteen seasons. He was a strong character, "the Prophet" and the "Lion of Judah" were two of his pseudonyms, and sometimes he resorted to strong language, but Somerset was a happy side. He was an excellent all-round batsman who liked to get on the front foot like the players of old, but if the situation needed a long studied innings, he could oblige. When he was coming to the end of his career, at the ripe age of 46, he hit centuries in both innings in a County match. He often fielded in a homburg hat, to protect his head from the sun, and positioned himself close in at silly point or better still at silly mid-off, where he could contemplate the batsman with a look which was destined to make them feel at least uncomfortable and at worst downright terrified. If the batsman played with care, his gaze would become pitying, as though they weren't fit to be at the crease. Robertson-Glasgow was convinced that he stared some of the more self-conscious batsmen back into the pavilion. One wonders what he would have made of the present-day "sledging", and indeed whether he would have indulged. I like to think that he would not. There is a limit, and that would have been beneath John Daniell, far too crude and unsophisticated. There are many excuses which batsmen put forward for getting out, but the Daniell favourite was a masterpiece, whenever he was caught in the deep, trying to be a latter-day Gilbert Jessop. *"Why can't that ruddy captain keep his fielders where he put 'em"*, would be his moan.

As the years unfolded, the combination of White and Daniell was to Somerset what White and Chapman later became to England. Daniell, positioned close in on the off, picked up a hat-full of catches off White and made many wonderful stops. It is not a place for the faint-hearted to field, and occasionally when White erred with a half-volley which was driven at high-speed straight through Daniell, he would look at White with an expression which needed no words to convey his feelings. So John Daniell trusted White's accuracy (most of the time!), and it recalls the observation of one of J.C.'s colleagues when commenting on his extraordinary accuracy. He bowled only about six bad balls a season, and most of those were in the nets in April! I expect the same slight exaggeration has been said about other bowlers, but it probably applies more appropriately to White than the others.

Another stalwart J.C. would meet as he started his career was Ernest Robson, a Yorkshireman who played first for Cheshire and then was spirited away to Somerset where he played for the County from 1895 to 1923. Robson was a professional and an all-rounder, though perhaps favouring the bowling for he was required to bowl often for very long spells. He would be described as right-hand medium pace and could keep an immaculate length, but also had the ability to make them move away from the bat very late. Jack Hobbs said that he feared no bowler of this kind more than Robson. Many who were in a position to know thought that he was most unlucky never to be selected for his country. His demeanour may have had something to do with that, because it is often the pushy ones who get to the front in all walks of life, and Ernest Robson was the very antithesis of self-promotion. He was a "nice" man, totally even-tempered. He was almost embarrassed whenever he claimed a wicket (which was frequently), and would belittle his achievement by stating that he had been lucky and explaining how the batsman should have played the ball. Robertson-Glasgow wondered whether even his family discovered what lay beneath that imperturbable exterior, and so I thought I would try to find out for his son Victor (no mean local cricketer himself) still lives in Taunton. Vic looked at me mystified that I should be asking such a question. There was nothing beneath that exterior. Ernest Robson was exactly as he appeared, what you saw was what you got. That must set him apart from many men.

When Robson joined Somerset from Cheshire, he had to spend two years qualifying for the County. During that time he played in club matches, bowled to the other players in the nets, and helped with the groundsman's work. He had learned these latter skills when with Cheshire. Somerset were never flush with money, and Vic recalls that after the war (1914-1918), Sammy Woods asked his father if he would look after the wickets. It was normal for him to arrive early on the morning of a match and prepare the wicket and then to bowl and bat in the match, including doing the work of marking the pitch between innings etc.

Ernest Robson was the first Somerset professional to score a thousand runs in a season and the first to score a century. He once took a hat-trick against Yorkshire which included both Wilfred Rhodes and George Hirst. He played for Somerset until he was 53, when he could still hit a six with nothing more than what appeared to be a forward push. He then qualified as an umpire, but before he could stand in even his first match, he died of cancer in Bristol hospital.

Sammy Woods, reminiscing with the News Editor of the Daily Express concerning the Somerset versus Surrey match at the Oval in 1900 stated, *"We beat Surrey twice that year which wasn't so unusual in those days, I had ptomaine poisoning - a bad gargle, I expect me dear - but I was keeping an end up when Robson came in. I said 'Look here Robbie, play yourself in and get some runs. I can't, I'm too weak, but I can stick in.' He said 'Very good sir, you attend to your end and I'll look after mine'. Can you believe it. He hit Richardson for three fours in his first over, and Lockwood for another three fours in his second over. That's playing yourself in! He got the best hundred on a bad wicket that I've ever seen, and when Surrey went in again he took 5 for 26 and they were all out for a hundred. Capable fellow Robbie, me dear; he was good enough for an Australian tour."*

Vic, with a good deal of pleasure, I thought, took me for a trip down memory lane. He recalled that his father regarded A.C. Russell of Essex as the best batsman he faced. He always thought that you had a chance with Jack Hobbs early in his innings, but if you missed out - watch out! He remembered that Harry Fearnley, the old Taunton groundsman, had one season when he thought that he would try to add a little colour to the ground and constructed flowerbeds outside the boundary but inside the surrounding picket fence. The line of the wicket was such that the flowerbed in front of the pavilion gathered anything which evaded the wicket-keeper. M.D. Lyon, keeping wicket, used to say when he missed one, *"That's another for the flora."* Vic recalls the absolute silence that reigned as batsman faced bowler, and when the early evening news vendor appeared with his advertising cries, a united "hush" would be demanded from the watching crowd.

Vic recalled that the toffs not only had their own cricket grounds but also sported their own blazers, which they provided for all the team.

Ernest Robson had other talents, and he played full-back for Stockport County and Derby County. The Taunton School magazine records the details of a football match played on Jarvis' field at Taunton in aid of the funds for Taunton and Somerset Hospital. The match was between Mr.E. Robson's XI versus Local Schools. E. Robson played full-back for the side which the magazine christened the Robsonians and the evergreen Sammy Woods played centre-forward. He had caps for England at cricket and rugby, and there is little doubt, all-round sportsman as he was, that he would have played for England at soccer if that had been his chosen direction. In spite of this show of talent, the Schools won by three goals to two.

Robson had many glorious days on the cricket field and we shall hear about some of them when he bowled in harness with J.C., but he probably considered his exploits against the Australians as some of his best. In 1896 he took 6 for 22 at Taunton and thirteen years later at Bath, he took 8 for 35 including Trumper, Noble, Gregory, Armstrong, and Bardsley. Wow!

A tradition which has survived since Bradman first went to Taunton with the Australian tourists is for them to be served wortleberry pie at the Castle Hotel - apparently it was a favourite dish of the great man. Two years ago, when they arrived early in the season to play Somerset, there was consternation at the Castle as the wortleberries weren't yet in season. Guess who saved the day, with five pounds of berries picked from the Quantocks and put down the previous year? Yes, Vic Robson! His Dad would have liked that.

Another professional to greet Jack White at his first match for the County would have been Len Braund. Len played for London County before removing to Somerset, and he was a genuine all-rounder. He was a man of flare, who when the mood was on him was an excellent raconteur on matters of cricket. He played for England on no less than 23 occasions, and in one series of Tests in Australia he scored a fine century and then followed it up by taking 8 wickets for 81 in one innings with leg-breaks of nearly medium pace. On his first appearance for England, against South Africa at Lord's, he made 104. He is particularly remembered for a wonderful catch he once made at fine-leg, when he was actually fielding at slip! But, best of all, he is remembered as the man who refused a second benefit match at Taunton, because he said he couldn't afford it! Goodness knows what happened on the first occasion.

Off the field of play, at this time, hoary chestnuts as they have become over the years, were starting their lives. One such was the tea interval. The tea interval had been a comparatively recent introduction, and it was not received with universal acclaim, least of all by the spectators. It was described as moral slackness on the part of the cricketers that they should require such an interval. Of course, the seating for the spectators at that time was rudimentary and there was doubtless a degree of resentment that the players were enjoying themselves whilst the spectators waited "tenderly". There was an occasion involving the visiting Australian tourists when tea was taken at the allotted time, with nine wickets down. Unfortunately, on the resumption of play, the new man lasted but briefly, occasioning a further break of ten minutes between the innings. One "city gentleman" expressed the view that the tea interval should be abolished, a pail of water and ice and oatmeal carried round the field of play at 4.30 for the benefit of those cricketers who did not appreciate the advantages of cherishing a "righteous thirst" until the dinner hour.

It was argued by the advocates of tea intervals that most other occupations then enjoyed such, and that these intervals were necessary both to revive the inner man and also as a short social interval stimulus. The matter reached international proportions when it was observed that the custom in the Dominions was to drink tea with all meals and to receive it in the field of work as a necessary refreshment on a hot afternoon. It was even suggested that Australian cricketers were known to have a bad patch mid-way through the afternoon as a result of wanting tea when it was not quite ready. It might have been argued by England that that was a good reason for NOT having an interval, but these were the "Golden Years", and such thoughts were untenable. In view of England's increasing difficulty in being able to beat the Aussies, it is something which the current English administration should perhaps put on their agenda for consideration.

It must be remembered that the game was gradually becoming more and more professionally based and as such required income. Somewhat reluctantly, therefore, the needs of the spectators had to be taken into account. Indeed, on the question of the tea interval, some Counties actually resolved to abolish it and did so for a season or two. All very strange really. As a spectator I have always welcomed the tea interval as an opportunity to attend to the needs of life, to rest and revive a flagging posterior, and for numerous other reasons.

Inclement weather will always be a hazard which taxes the patience of cricket administrator and spectator alike. There were discussions on how to entertain the spectator during these wretched intervals of no play, and musical innovations were considered. The Times correspondent, E. B. Osborn, considering the introduction of bands to entertain the spectators in 1910, deplored the experiment in this direction which had already taken place at that most hallowed of grounds -Lord's itself. He considered that the old adage *"Don't mix your arts"* should apply, stating that cricket is a complete art in itself - epic, or dramatic, or lyric, as the man and the moment might determine. He applauded the action of Mr. C.I. Thornton, going in to bat at Scarborough and ordering the band to stop playing. They complied with his wishes, but in the ensuing silence Mr. Thornton failed his cause and supporters by being out for a duck. The following batsman did not wish to tempt fate a second time and the band therefore continued merrily on its way. A few grounds provided bands, but mostly on festival occasions and even then in the meal intervals, but it was not an innovation which caught on. It is only in rcent years that taped music has started to intrude into the action whilst players are actually on the field of play, though still, fortunately, not whilst the players are actually performing their tasks of bowling, batting and fielding.

Referring to Osborn's *"Don't mix your Arts"*, I can't help wondering how he would have reacted to a present day visit to one of the North American stadiums of sport, where everything "goes"! A recent experience of the Calgary Flames ice-hockey "Saddledome" (the building is shaped like a saddle) in Alberta alerted me to the possibilities of "things to come", and these are not necessarily bad, although Osborn might not have agreed with me.

This fantastic 40,000 seat, entirely covered, stadium has as its main attraction the watching of major league ice-hockey between teams wonderfully featured as "the Flames", "the Oilers", etc. The hockey is played out with many stirring accompaniments, such as huge gushes of flame every time the Flames score a goal, and intermittent requests for the paying customers to produce "Noise", encouraged by growing displays of the word

"Noise" on huge screens which are suspended from the roof of the stadium. These same screens keep the customers informed of a multitude of other happenings, such as the highlights of play in the day's major baseball and football games. Just imagine going to a Lord's Test and being shown the highlights of the play at Wimbledon in the tea interval. M.C.C. members should not be reading this, there will be too many heart attacks. But that is only the start of it.

From every corner of the Saddledome, fast food is dispensed and stalls sell everything from drinks to lottery tickets, sports clothing to sunglasses. The corridors around the arena are full of purchasers even whilst the play on the ice is in progress. On the ice itself, there are no intervals from a continuing entertainment. As soon as the hockey players depart the ice, comedians and jugglers appear. Amusing competitions are played out, the latest models of new cars parade the ice, celebrities are introduced, randomly chosen fans receive exciting prizes. . . . . .

It is non-stop entertainment. Watch out cricket. Coloured clothing and white (yellow) balls are only for starters! But seriously, this type of introduction may be exactly what is needed to keep cricket afloat and to make it palatable to a wider audience. The powers that run cricket had better start exercising their minds or they might find themselves without customers. It might not be wise to solely depend on the income from selling themselves to television companies.

All of these innovations will be of no interest to the elite band of panama-hatted elderly gentlemen who simply find the cricket conducive to an afternoon's nap in the warm sun.

An associated subject is the English weather. Too often supporters are expected to turn up at a match when the weather is uncertain to say the least. They pay their admission monies and then it is in the lap of the Gods whether they see six hours play or six minutes. There is usually no attempt whatsoever to provide alternative entertainment. A select few retire to inner sanctums or hospitality suites, the remainder receive a corporate two fingers. More consideration is a must if cricket grounds are to be filled - or even half-filled.

At the time of J.C. 's introduction to County cricket, in a changing world, Lord Hawke, that great Yorkshire captain and disciplinarian, attempted to explain in a written article in The Times the definition of an amateur as opposed to a professional. It was a subject which was causing troubles in sports other than cricket at the time, notably soccer and rugby.

It was a tricky subject, even Lord Hawke admitted that, though in his own mind the situation was quite clear. It is amusing that he saw the difficulties as being in other sports, whilst cricket, presumably on a higher plane, allegedly experienced no such problems, or *"viewed them with a calm indifference".* He felt that as cricket had had an acknowledged and welcomed professionalism for nigh on two hundred year, *"May we not rather assume that we have passed through the scathing fires, and may we not without arrogance suggest that what may seem indifference is in truth the wisdom of experience, and possibly worth studying, and that from our store of experiences may be gleaned some facts that may help other pastimes to treat the problem with less rancour?"*

Some might describe that as pompous poppycock. Lord Hawke informed his readership that there was a definition of the amateur in the M.C.C.'s committee records to the effect that, *"That cricketer is not an amateur who makes a profit out of playing the game".* Lord Hawke pointed out that the well-meant definition lacked one essential, the definition of what is profit. He did not see any great need to have a marked distinction between amateurs and professionals which rested on financial reward, as a much clearer distinction is at hand, namely the daily avocation, the profession of the individual.

What Lord Hawke was arguing, nay stating, after all he was Lord Hawke not some two-bit professional, was that it did not matter if certain men received cash as wages and others received it as expenses, the crucial decision as to whether a man was a professional was did he spend all his time playing cricket in the season, and that was his one and only source of income. If so, he was a professional. If, however, his main source of income came from elsewhere outside cricket, he was an amateur. This did not mean that he should not receive remuneration for his cricketing "expenses". Then we come to another lack of definition. What are expenses?

Having disposed of the financial side of amateurism and professionalism, Lord Hawke explained that the social differences were entirely a matter of being courteous to one's hosts. He must have had his tongue in his cheek here. If the host club chose to provide separate dressing rooms and sitting rooms for the two disciplines, then as true Englishmen, one accepted the position without demur. Similarly, if the host club said that the professionals should enter the field of play through one gate and the amateurs through another, so be it. A matter of no importance - at least not to the amateurs.

Lord Hawke pointed out that all the players dressed alike on the field of play, except that some of the amateurs chose not to wear a cap. He didn't say what would have happened if one of the professionals had preferred to go bare-headed.

So, concluded Lord Hawke, the professional knows his position and knowing that the amateur regards him as his comrade, he has no need to trouble his head any further. Both disciplines have for some years past been striving to raise the status of the professional cricketer, and successfully; and the higher he has risen the closer have become the bonds of comradeship between him and the amateur, and the rude and abusive professional will now be avoided by those of his own profession as markedly as by amateurs! How could he write that. The answer is that he could nearly a century ago. It would probably have been received as enlightened thinking, and if anyone took exception to it, it would probably have been the amateur rather than the professional.

The position on status at the time is put into perspective when one remembers that Lord Hawke was one of the best captains as regards looking after the needs of his professionals. He may have been a stickler for discipline, but he was in the lead when it came to finding ways to improve the financial rewards and conditions of his men. I suppose that was it, he wanted them to be good employees and to be treated as such - but social equality, that was something else. Things don't change that much, do they? As regards the rude and abusive professional, they did exist. The most noteworthy case was the celebrated Yorkshire and England all-rounder, Bobby Peel. He had performed heroically for county and country on numerous occasions, but it was too much for Lord Hawke when he drunkenly relieved himself one day on the field of play. He was despatched forth, never to play again - and some people thought that streakers were a symptom of the modern age!

The differentiation between amateurs and professionals continued long after Lord Hawke, until 1962 in fact; and the continuance of different social strata in England is evident in all walks of life, albeit less by chance of birth than previously. An amusing example occurred when the late Field Marshall Montgomery visited Lord's. The cultured tones of the announcer spoke of play commencing not starting, and the rain ceasing not stopping - I wonder if foreign visitors would pick up the slight nuances - but then requested that a doctor should attend someone via the back door of the pavilion. The Field Marshall later wrote to the M.C.C.and suggested that in such circumstances in the future, it might be preferable to refer to the rear door rather than back door. It was not quite the thing for a professional person to be treated as though he was a tradesman. One can't help wondering whether a surgeon, supposedly on a higher plane than a mere doctor, would have been permitted to use the front door, or whatever a front door is called in higher parlance.

And so, Jack White's county cricketing career started (or commenced - he was an amateur), and incidentally according to his son, Tom, J.C. was quite at ease with the differentiation between amateurs and professionals, and had no particular kites to fly or causes to pursue on the subject. When Tom remonstrated with his father on the iniquities of separate dressing rooms etc. etc., he was treated as most young men have been treated by their fathers at some time in their adolescence, with the immortal phrase, *"Oh, you don't understand."* And that was the end of it.

J.C. was picked to play for Somerset at the age of eighteen at Bath for the May 20th-22nd, 1909 fixture against Lancashire. He scored 4 and 5 not out and bowled 0 for 39 off 13 overs and 1 for 8 off two overs. His first wicket was that of Huddleston, caught (as so many would be) by Daniell. Daniell scored 121 not out and 35 and Somerset lost by the small margin of 9 runs. White also played in the next match against Yorkshire at Bradford. Yorkshire declared at 345 for 9 and White had 0 for 43 off 13 overs. Somerset scored 21 for 1 and the match was drawn so presumably the weather interfered. White had two more firsts - his first wide, and his first catch, taking E.J. Radcliffe off the bowling of Braund. He was not asked to play again that season and thus his analysis for his first season of County cricket was 1 wicket for 90 runs off 28 overs, and 9 runs at an average of 4.5. Not an auspicious start.

In 1910, he played 17 innings, usually batting at no. 11, and was not out 6 times, scoring 112 runs with a highest score of 23 and an average of 10. 18. He bowled 140 overs, 13 maidens, and took 8 wickets for 514 runs at an average of 64. 25. Not a lot better than the previous year. Then, it was a case of *"Don't call us, we'll call you."*

The subject of "imported" cricketers is often thought of as a modern phenomenon, together with all the arguments which it engenders. The stifling of the progress of homegrown talent, the unfairness of fielding established players from other countries rather than relying on young men of English parentage, and the undermining of careers for those young men. Yet, in 1909, there was already argument and counter-argument raging.

Middlesex were supposedly one of the main culprits, and their position and results in the preceeding years was largely attributed to their engagement of those two Australian stalwarts, Trott and Tarrant. The latter was used as an example to demonstrate the point by those who were opposed to allowing colonials to play in England, even though they had to serve a qualifying period. In one match against Gloucestershire, the game was finished within the first day, almost entirely due to the efforts of Tarrant. He opened the batting for Middlesex and carried his bat through the innings. He then proceeded to bowl throughout both Gloucestershire innings, taking thirteen wickets for 67 runs. He had dominated the match to the exclusion of his team-mates, and this was not a good thing for either them or for English cricket.

Some thought that a colonial amateur could be allowed to play in the English County Championship after the given qualifying period, but for a professional to do so was a flagrant instance of commercialism in cricket and should not be allowed. The topic did not affect White because Somerset were always short of cash, and therefore employed the very minimum of professionals. A good amateur was worth his weight in gold to Somerset.

It was a long wait for White before he received the call to assist Somerset once more. Suddenly, in 1913 he blossomed. Called back to the team, after two years in the wilderness, he demonstrated that he had not wasted those two years and that his village and club cricket had honed his bowling talents to a level which would mean that he would never be dropped again. I would love to know whether he used to visit Ernest Tyler during that time for more coaching. I feel certain he would, and he was a member of the Old Tauntonians so presumably he would have had the opportunity. He definitely played for the Somerset Stragglers Cricket Club which had been formed in 1900 following the proposal that *"An Amateur Cricket Club for the County of Somerset be founded."* The club shared the County ground with the Somerset C.C.C. J.C. was in the team on the 11th July 1911 when the visitors were a Clergy XI. He took several wickets, but his analysis may not have been one of his best, because the Clergy scored 453 for 9 dec. The Stragglers replied with 458 for 1, made in two hours twenty minutes! 911 runs were scored in 6 hours that day. Must have been a batsman's wicket!

White returned to playing with the Stragglers when his County career finished and his best performances for them appear to have been in the twilight of his cricketing life. He took 9 wickets in an innings twice, including 9 for 9 against Queen's College, Taunton on June 2nd 1938. Apparently he never went on the Stragglers' "tours", which appear to have been jolly affairs. On one tour to the Channel Isles, the wicket-keeper had a day-trip to St. Malo and was brought back on a hurdle. His story the next day was that he met someone who he had not seen since the Battle of the Marne in 1914. A footnote to this incident recalls that the day before he went on his trip he conceded 61 byes, afterwards he kept very well!

Returning to the subject of County cricket, White finished the 1913 season at the top of the Somerset bowling averages with 772.3 overs, 208 maidens, and 93 wickets for 1832 runs at an average of 19.69! He was top catcher with 19. His batting was less prolific and he scored 171 runs, highest score 40 at an average of 7.43. Unfortunately Somerset didn't reflect his fortunes, and they won only two matches and finished bottom of the County table.

In the following year, White again topped the Somerset bowling averages, with 83 wickets at a cost of only 15.11 runs each. His value to the County is demonstrated by the fact that Robson, who was second in the averages, took 78 wickets at 27.03 runs each, almost twice as many runs per wicket. The local newspaper bemoaned the fact that White could not have played more often. This point should be taken into account also when comparing the number of wickets which he took in his career against those taken by others, particularly the professionals. He took more than most people, as will be seen later, and topped the hundred on a regular basis, but Phil Edmonds stated in an article that he never exceeded the 200 wickets in a season. True, but as an amateur there were times when his farming took precedence over his cricket, therefore the number of games in which he played was limited.

With the advent of the first world war, cricket took a back seat for a few years whilst man indulged in more barbarian pursuits. It was the end of what many still regard as "the Golden Age" of cricket. It had been a time when it was normal for a bowler to apologise for dropping one short or bowling down the legside. Conan Doyle, the creator of Sherlock Holmes, had played in his only first class match, and had taken the wicket of W.G. Grace and proceeded to write a nineteen stanza epic in commemoration of his triumph. In 1905 Joe Darling, the Australian captain, refused to appeal against poor light in a match which they were losing, saying that Australia had been outplayed and harboured no desire to escape by such a route.

Imagine that today! He would have been relieved of the captaincy forthwith, ridiculed by the press, the experts, and his own governing body alike, and cast into the wilderness for evermore.

It was a time when, if there were any bounders on the cricket field, they were of the innocent kind, such as the great W.G. himself, who simply did not like being out and considered that his genius which gave pleasure to thousands should be rewarded by not only clapping the hands together but also by placing one of them in the back-pocket. The stories of W.G.'s dislike of dismissal are legion and he would not hesitate to try to bully his way into a longer stay at the crease. There was the day when the bowler caught him plumb in front of his stumps and the appeal for lbw was upheld by the umpire. W.G. protested that he had played the ball with his bat. Unfortunately he had omitted to note that the ball had proceeded from his pads into the hands of the adjacent fielder. *"All right,"* said the disgruntled umpire, *"you are out caught then"*. Even W.G. had no answer to that. Of course, the best way to get W.G. out without any room for doubt or discussion was to bowl him. Sammy Woods did so quite comprehensively on one occasion at Lord's after he had suffered a number of refused appeals. The off and middle stumps were knocked clean out of the ground. W.G. surveyed the damage, hesitated, and then started to leave the arena only to hear Woods saying, *"Don't go yet, there's still one standing"*. W.G. 's response isn't recorded!

The Golden Age had witnessed some of the most ferocious hitting of all times. Gilbert Jessop, only 5ft. 7ins. tall and called "The Croucher" because of his stance, had hit 53 centuries, of which 15 were scored in under the hour! He holds the record for the fastest century against the Australians, 75 minutes at the Oval in 1902. Incidentally, our hero J.C. White took Jessop's wicket twice in the latter's last match.

Whilst White was enjoying his early sabbatical from first class cricket in 1911 after only two seasons; he was lucky enough to avoid Ted Alletson of Nottinghamshire. Ted was a massive man with an arm-span of 6 ft. 6 ins. If he was from Nottingham, it is likely that he would have enjoyed an occasional day out at the sea at Skegness, the traditional haunt of the Midlanders on holiday. His liking for a bathe was satisfied at Hove one day, before he went out to bat at No. 9, would you believe. He proceeded to hit 189 in 90 minutes. He "dawdled" over his first 50, which took nearly an hour - I expect he lost the strike; he then hit 142 runs in 40 minutes! At one point the small boys were searching outside the ground for five balls, all dispatched thither in quick succession. We will not divulge the names of the bowlers. Just imagine them as he came out to bat at No. 9, thinking that their task was almost finished! Incidentally, Ted was batting on that day with only one sound wrist.

The war years were to claim many of these heroes, many injured to an extent which prevented them from playing again, others who were savagely dispatched to some Elysian field in the sky. One of the former was the ex-Warwickshire captain, F.R. Foster, with whom Douglas Jardine consorted years later in 1932 before he set forth as captain of England to Australia with the express and sole purpose of bringing back the Ashes. That was, of course, the notorious Bodyline series, and Jardine consulted Foster as he had been an exponent of fast leg theory, a theory which was based on aiming the ball at or just outside the leg stump, cramping the batsman's ability to play on the offside, and packing the leg-side with fielders waiting for the catches. If the batsman failed to get bat on ball, or failed to move himself smartly out of the way, he could suffer a fearful whack on the body. In modern cricket, although protected to some degree by rules which limit the number of balls above shoulder height and similar devices, the batsman is considered fair game for a little intimidation of this nature.

In the era of the Golden Age before 1914, a more gentlemanly attitude was prevalent and, indeed, as has been stated earlier, bowlers would apologise for such activities. How then do we equate Foster's use of fast leg theory with the nobleness of those times? There are several explanations. Firstly, Foster was not a fast bowler and therefore his use of the theory might produce wickets but it was unlikely to cause injury to the batsmen. Secondly, it was the end of the Golden Age, and therefore a more competitive above all else attitude may have been starting to appear. Thirdly, in the same way that one remembers all the good things of one's childhood and not the bad things, or remembers the long hot summers and not the wet ones, perhaps the noble acts of the Golden Years are recounted and not the ignoble deeds or misdemeanours.

All of *"the glorious dead"* are remembered each year, officially on the 11th November and at other times by those dear ones they left behind. In the case of the cricketers who laid down their lives, some were fortunate enough already to have recorded deeds on the field of play which have earned them a place in the records and history of the game. A.E.J. Collins is one such example, albeit as a schoolboy cricketer. In 1899, at the age of fourteen, playing for his house at Clifton College, he made 628 not out over a period of 5 afternoons. . . . . . before bravely giving his life at the Battle of Ypres.

The 1915 Wisden Cricketers' Almanack listed 44 war casualties, the 1916 edition 285, the 1917 edition 500, the 1918 edition 400 (and 84 from previous years), and the 1919 edition 330 (and 46 from previous years). Dr. W.G. Grace also died in this period.

E. W. Hornung, who was the brother-in-law of Conan Doyle and who created Raffles the cricketing burglar, wrote in 1915:

> *"No Lord's this year; no silken lawn on which*
> *A dignified and dainty throng meanders.*
> *The Schools take guard upon a firier pitch*
> *Somewhere in Flanders. "*

While J.C. Squire, another of the cricket-loving poets of the time, wrote, *"'My God,' said God, 'I've got my work cut out.'"*

4.

THIS AND THAT

WHEN FIRST CLASS cricket resumed after the war, Somerset's finances were in little better state than when the war commenced. In 1914, they had been obliged to pacify the bank with a shilling fund which raised £500. One of the economy measures adopted was to rely on amateurs for the majority of the team. Two regular professionals only were engaged, and they were both old reliables of pre-war years. Len Braund had more or less given up bowling, but still provided some much-needed solidity at the heart of the batting. Ernest Robson, now in his late forties, was still game to play the role of stock-bowler and provide some useful runs in addition.

John Daniell, known as "The Prophet", was the captain and as a University man himself, he recruited a talented collection of young men from Cambridge and Oxford without paying too much attention to the qualifying rules.

J.C. White had by now become a regular and essential member of the side, whenever his farming activities permitted. These did not appear to interrupt his cricketing too often, and that was no doubt due to his father's generosity in holding the fort.

Most of the Somerset matches were played at Taunton on the County ground which is as near to the centre of the town as any County ground in the country. It stands beside the river Tone, and is dominated on one side by church towers. Across the river to the north and west lie the Quantock Hills, where it is rumoured Sammy Woods used to conceal caches of liquor. He then invited a friend or acquaintance to run or walk with him over the hills, and when they were pleasantly perspiring, he would innocently enquire whether a bottle of something refreshing might be appreciated. His pleasure was in observing the look of incredulity on the face of his companion as he dived behind a tree or into undergrowth and re-appeared holding two bottles.

The Taunton ground today is much changed from when J.C. knew it, but still has a delightful homely atmosphere, and a lovely mish-mash of different buildings surrounding the playing area. Large new pavilions stand in close proximity to smaller picturesque stands, and there must be more to look at and study than on most grounds. Nobody should be bored on the Taunton ground during a stoppage in play, there is so much to occupy the mind. That is providing the stoppage is not too long of course. Apparently the Taunton Athletic Co. secured the ground in 1885, and a year later the newly re-organised County Cricket Club acquired the lease. Then began the work of covering the running track and erection of the first of the stands. The Supporters' Club has been a tremendous support for many years and has played a valuable role in allowing the expansion of facilities and updating and modernisation where thought appropriate or essential from an amenity or safety need. Of course, the introduction of the new sometimes necessitates the removal of the old, and one such loss which few would have lamented, but which Jack White would have remembered, was the stable in the north-west corner which housed the horse which pulled the roller and the mower. - now the way Vic Robson tells it, you would have thought that his father pulled the roller and mower himself!

This lovely ground, which had been the scene of W. G. Grace's century of centuries in 1895 (he celebrated with champagne and then proceeded to 288 in 320 minutes), and later was to witness Jack Hobbs surpassing the great man's record of 126 centuries, had the indignity (or perhaps it should be honour) thrust upon it to become an army camp during the First World War. Fittingly, it was the Australian army, the old ground wasn't going to accommodate just anybody. Army vehicles and plant were stored on the playing surface and it took a long time after the war before all the ruts and wheel-tracks had been eliminated. When peace was restored to Europe the ground was handed back and it was in a state of some dereliction. Rabbits were abundant, and Sammy Woods wondered to whom to turn. Well, of course, who else but Ernest Robson who had a twelve bore and a licence. No sooner said than done.

The Telegraph suggests that in the pre-war years Somerset was probably the worst side in the Championship, customarily fielding teams of ageing, low-grade amateurs - oh dear - and supports this allegation by pointing out that they finished in the bottom three in each of the five pre-war years. Fairly indisputable evidence, I suppose. At least our hero was a member of the team in only two of those years.

John Daniell and his team, including White, embarked on the 1919 season with the County still sorely troubled by money problems, but in the spirit of the game these were brushed aside whilst play began. Almost in the first match, controversy reared its head and Somerset together with Sussex wrote themselves into the cricketing history books. In a game which had looked as though it was going Sussex's way, there was suddenly a revival of Somerset's fortunes. The ninth Sussex wicket fell with the scores level. H.J. Heygate of Sussex had been injured and had not intended batting. Somewhat belatedly, the Sussex captain decided to throw him into the breach, and colleagues set about fitting his pads over his civilian clothes. As he emerged onto the field of play, one of the umpires declared him *"out of time"*, the only instance in first class cricket. The relevant Law 45 states that the incoming batsman is allowed two minutes when the umpire calls *"play"*; the side refusing to play shall lose the match. So much for the chivalrous Golden Age, that had finished with the war. There was now, shall we say, a more aggressive attitude prevailing.

In actual fact, it was one of the umpires who decided that the game was over, the old Surrey professional Street, and he pulled up the stumps. The two captains were both amenable to the game being continued to a conclusion. The second umpire was the ex-Gloucestershire bowler Roberts, and he would not intervene. As the scores were level, the umpires declared the match a tie. According to the Law, a team which is "timed out" shall lose the game, but Sussex had already scored as many runs as Somerset, so how could they be adjudged to have lost! It was a situation which the Law had not foreseen.

In July of that year J.C. White hit the national headlines for what was to be the first of many occasions. The venue was Bath and it was the first of the festival matches. Worcestershire were the visitors. Somerset batted first and scored 241. There was a long interruption for rain and it was a quarter to three in the afternoon before Worcestershire could start their innings. As far as they were concerned it was obviously still far too early, for in one and a half hours they were all back in the hutch, skittled for 67. White had taken 8 wickets for 36 runs off 17 overs. Asked to follow on, Worcestershire tried again with little more success than on the previous occasion. This time they amassed 78 runs and White took 8 wickets for 47 runs off 19.4 overs. The visitors had been beaten by an innings and 96 runs. It was sometimes said in later years that Jack White was at his most dangerous on hard dry wickets. He could bowl a bit on a sticky dog also.

Amazingly, in the next festival match against Derbyshire, it was White's bowling partner who did the damage. Ernest Robson had a 7 wickets for 19 runs analysis in Derby's second innings.

That year, and for that year only, for thereafter it was rescinded, matches were scheduled for two days. The reason was that the powers that be decided that spectators in the post-war era would not be prepared or have the time to support three day fixtures. Perhaps that was the spur which hurried messrs. White and Robson in their unseemly haste to dispose of the opposition in the Bath festival matches.

In the review of the cricketing year in the County Gazette, amongst other matters, the lack of accuracy in throwing to the wicket-keeper was criticised; and coincidentally this same topic was referred to in the M.C.C. memorial volume to the late W.G. Grace. The subject of throwing recalls the occasion when W.G. challenged the Oxonian V.T. Hill that for a sovereign he could not throw a ball 100 yards three times, alternately with and against the wind. They tossed to decide whether two of the throws should be with or against the wind. Hill won, and in a light breeze, with the assistance of the wind, he threw the ball 119 yards and 2 feet. Unfortunately, he could manage only 91 yards against it. W.G. was delighted and quickly demanded the money. Knowing what we do now of W.G.'s reputation, there is little doubt who the winner of that wager was going to be.

The end of the 1919 season found Jack White in the highly commendable position of third in the national bowling averages with 128 wickets for 1,913 runs at an average of 14.94, taken from 880 overs. He had reached a height which he was to maintain for many seasons to come.

In the close season, Lord Harris took the chair at the meeting of the Counties Advisory Committee, with representatives present from the M.C.C., all the first-class counties and the Minor Counties Association. The proceedings were private, and at the end of the meeting information regarding the results of the different motions was supplied to the press and the general public. The chief decision was that, for the next season, three-day matches would be reinstated so that cricket would carry on very much as before the war. The fact that about half of the games in 1919 had ended (or failed to end) in a draw must have weighed heavily in the voting.

The twenties decade dawned to persuasion by Australia for England - or perhaps that should read M.C.C. - to send a team to Australia to contend the Ashes. England had hardly recovered from the war and were not too keen, but it had been nine years since the two protagonists had faced each other, and therefore the request was obliged. Australia had weathered the war well, and cricket there had become more popular than ever, with massive scores, sometimes in inter-state matches exceeding a thousand runs per innings, matched by equally large and vociferous crowds. The game in England was also relatively well supported, which scotched the pessimism of the Jeremiahs who were predicting that it would be replaced by baseball. Jack Hobbs was acknowledged as the best batsman in the world - at least by the English - and the opening partnership of Hobbs and Sutcliffe was supreme. Unfortunately England had lost a number of her best bowlers in the war years and had not yet identified their replacements. England went to Australia and suffered the ignominy of a 5-0 thrashing, being beaten in all Tests for the first time, and worse, all by substantial margins.

At home, the County Championship was as keenly contested as ever and in his last year as captain of Middlesex, Sir Pelham Warner, as he was to become, had the great satisfaction of leading his county to the top of the table. "Plum" Warner may have finished his stint on the field of play, but there were many more years of involvement at the top for this eighteenth child of a Trinidadian attorney-general who had arrived in England in 1887, schooled at Rugby, University Oxford, and was called to the bar but never practised as cricket was his life. He played for Oxford, Middlesex and England, captaining all at some stage, and he later became Deputy Secretary and then President of M.C.C., manager of their touring sides, including the bodyline series. He combined his playing career with journalism and became cricket correspondent for the Morning Post, and he founded his own magazine, The Cricketer. His longevity and his position at the hub of cricket, Lord's, for so long gave him a right to his patriarchial image in later years. But you can't please everybody, and he tended to retain certain attitudes which he had held fifty years previously, whilst the rest of the world had moved on. John Arlott once upset him when asked to address an audience and he included, *"For my part, I shall continue to speak of Dennis Compton as though he were my friend, and not as if he were my groom."* The roles of the amateur and the professional had been quite distinct throughout Sir Pelham's life, and it seems almost uncanny that he died on the day before M.C.C. took the decision to have done with the distinction for ever.

In every cricket year there are items of note and special interest, and in 1920 on the 15th May another great English captain of the future, Percy Chapman, was making his debut in first-class cricket, with 118 for Cambridge University against Essex. In Australia at the end of the year, Wilfred Rhodes became the first player ever to make 2000 runs and take 100 wickets in Test matches.

In Somerset, John Daniell had recruited to his side the Oxonian R.C. "Crusoe" Robertson-Glasgow, who acquired his agnomen after a match against Essex when he bowled one Charlie McGahey. J.W.H.T. - "Johnny won't hit today"- Douglas, the Essex captain, had asked McGahey how he was out and McGahey answered, *"I was bowled by an old. . . . . I thought was dead two thousand years ago, called Robinson Crusoe."* Robertson-Glasgow was a useful medium fast bowler, but he is remembered for his cricket journalism which was witty and original, punchy and entertaining. It is obvious when reading some writers that they have enjoyed their work, and Robertson-Glasgow comes into that class. Somerset has benefited from having him play for them, for he has left many stories of the county and the characters he met. A short read of a selection of his stories is sufficient to confirm that no county would have suited him better than Somerset. There was always a convivial atmosphere in the dressing room, time for a joke and a laugh, seriousness in their efforts but not in their countenances (except John Daniell fielding at silly point to a prospective rabbit).

Robertson-Glasgow recalls his first game, when Somerset's opponents were Hampshire, and not only was Lord Tennyson playing but also his valet-cum-wicket-keeper, Walter Livsey. Crusoe reports that they had three ducks between them, two to the master and one to the man. Every so often, when I think of that story, I can't help wondering how many Walter scored in his second innings, and whether the good lord was proud of him or resented his usurpation of the master's rightful position. In that match, Tennyson was caught off White in each innings. Every year at Taunton he would swear that he would hit Jack White for six, but the ground is a little bigger than it looks, and Jack White was a bowler with whom the best batsmen in the land learned not to trifle. Every year the ball would land safely in the deep fielder's hands.

Lord Tennyson had a reputation as a hitter, especially to fast bowling. He lived by the maxim that the harder they come, the harder they go. Robertson-Glasgow displays his genius of description when he says of Tennyson, *"in defence or attack, he could use a forward stroke which for sheer decision, I have never seen excelled."* A few descriptive sentences from R-G were sufficient that there was no need for the reader to attend the match, as he could visualise not only the player but the mood and temperament of the player and the kind of game that he was playing. He painted the picture with words more informatively than it could ever be done with colours. The story that R-G himself liked best about Tennyson was when in the West Indies a spectator was heard to ask with pleasing ambiguity: *"Will the good lord be making a second coming?"* Tennyson was the grandson of the famous Poet Laureate, but he said that all he could remember of him was a beard peering over the end of his bed.

Cricket was and is full of characters, the stories of whom, like a good wine, improve with keeping. One such character, who started his first class career just before Jack White, would never be known by his proper name, Elias Hendren, but replace the Elias with an alias, Patsy, and everyone knew of him. He was a professional who came up the hard way, together with his brother. Indeed, his brother could tell of the hardships of the average professional cricketer much better than Patsy, because he had nothing like the same success, and therefore did not qualify for the perks of Test and representative matches, and the security of winter work on overseas tours. They both signed for Middlesex, which in those days meant that they also signed for the M.C.C., Lord's being the home of both clubs. The story is told of how they would, together with their professional colleagues, report to the entrance gates to the ground each Spring to be met by the secretary of the M.C.C. who had two forms to sign, one for M.C.C. and one for Middlesex, and their wages for the first week.

Some attempt is made later in this book to define Jack White's attributes as a bowler, but none of the descriptions can outdo Patsy Hendren's. He said quite simply that Mr. White, he always called him that, made him feel more tired than when he batted against any other bowler. In a nutshell, the uncomplicated Patsy has it. White seldom bowled a bad ball, the batsman had to watch every single one or else he was back in the pavilion. That sort of concentration for, perhaps hour after hour, can be extremely exhausting.

In 1934 Patsy wrote a sort of cricketing autobiography, titled "Big Cricket". It cost two shillings and can be read in about two hours. It could not be described as a competitor to Cardus or Arlott, and there is little doubt that a ghost writer was not employed for the prose is simplicity itself, but it gives interesting insights into the thoughts and opinions of a professional of that era. When England recently dispensed with the services of Michael Atherton as her captain, there was a great debate concerning his successor. Patsy Hendren states quite categorically that in his opinion, the wicket-keeper is the best man to captain a side. Of all the players on the field, he is in the best position to judge what is happening. He can not only see how the pitch is playing, but by his own exertions knows how the pitch is playing. He can also see how comfortable the batsman is and what appears to worry him most. Most importantly, he can judge which bowler is likely to get a wicket and when someone is not quite on song. Patsy is almost as adamant that only in exceptional circumstances should a bowler be the captain. He did not think that a bowler/captain could avoid falling between the two stools of on the one hand having too much confidence in himself and therefore overbowling himself, and the alternative of being too modest and not bowling when it was in the team's interests that he should. So Patsy would probably have agreed with the appointment by of Alec Stewart to the captaincy of England - even though he does play for Surrey!

Patsy had a simple opinion of what is required to gain selection as a batsman for England, or for that matter for any representative side - HUNDREDS. It is the centuries which get written about and talked about, not the style of the batsman or anything else. Ninety is no good. That will receive a hard-luck story but cut no ice and will be soon forgotten. If a batsman is scoring hundreds the selectors have no choice but to pick him. He goes on to state that therefore the batsman who enjoys his cricket but wishes to get to the top must learn not to use certain strokes except in dire emergencies because sweet as such strokes may be to play, and in spite of the huge satisfaction they give, their risk factor is too great.

To illustrate one point in which Patsy was a firm believer, he tells the story of Bobby Abel, the old Surrey batter. He had batted all day and was out just before the close having scored over two hundred runs. A friend went to find him to congratulate him on a wonderful innings. He was nowhere to be found, until the friend located him in an out of the way room, bat in hand, in front of a full-length mirror. On being asked what he was doing, he replied that he was trying to work out *"how the deuce I got out to that ball"*. The moral and lesson is that a batsman should not simply glorify in his achievements, but more importantly should analyse his mistakes so that he can avoid them in the future. Wise counsel.

Patsy Hendren was the sort of fellow who was popular with players and supporters wherever he went. Bill Andrews of Somerset recalled the start of his career and his first visit to Lord's. With the Somerset side comprising mainly amateurs, and therefore housed separately, Bill was feeling rather lonely, but it wasn't long before Patsy sidled over and sat down beside him and made him feel much more at home. Bill hardly deserved this kindly friendship because in recounting the story he described Patsy as the ugliest man he had ever seen.

In Australia Patsy soon struck up a rapport with the cricket followers and he had the ability to give as good as he got with the barrackers, which immediately gave him status and made him acceptable. He recalls fielding on the boundary and one spectator asking why a certain individual had not come on tour. Patsy told him that they had selected only good-looking players. *"How in the world did they choose you then?"* came the response. After more backchat, a few overs later, Patsy was instructed to field elsewhere and Andy Sandham took his place on the same boundary. As Sandham arrived, the Aussies took one long look, then in chorus sang out, *"We want Hendren back"*. Sandham never did understand the joke.

The Australian supporters are almost as likely to give their own team the stick, particularly if things are not going their way. On the 1928/29 tour Hammond had a hatful of runs almost everywhere he went, and the crowd soon devised a ditty with which they pilloried their own bowlers every so often, chanting: *"You'll never get him out, you'll never get him out"*. They can of course be just as amusing, as at Adelaide in Jack White's great match, with Australia requiring few runs but having only one wicket left, when in a hushed moment a loan plaintive voice shrilled to Oldfield, *"Bertie, if you get the runs you'll surely go to heaven"*.

Another topic arose in Hendren's book which is, if anything, of even more interest in modern cricket than it was in his day, and that is the subject of the fielding side appealing. It is often discussed whether the fielders influence the umpires by their vociferous appeals, particularly if they all appeal in unison. It must be disconcerting for the umpire to know that all around are saying "out", even though he knows that they have a vested interest. He has to have the strongest resolve to contradict such opinion, particularly now that he is aware that all will be revealed ad nauseam on the television replays. There is more tendency for batsmen to query decisions given against them, if only by the mildest gesture or facial expression, and no wonder when they know that the fielders are out to get them by fair means or foul. Hendren recalls that the old Middlesex skipper, Gregor McGregor, never ever showed, by so much as a blink of the eyelid, that he was surprised at any decision given for or against him. One day an umpire gave McGregor out, and later it was discussed in the pavilion. The umpire said that he was a little worried by his decision, but after he had given it, he looked at McGregor who showed no sign of displeasure and therefore he was happy that he had been correct in his decision. Hendren was using the example to demonstrate his captain's quality of sportmanship, but surely it also demonstrates that the passive player is less likely to receive equal consideration as the noisy aggressive player. When winning is everything, it is going to be difficult preventing players from trying to gain an edge over their opponents, and aggressive appealing is likely to give them that edge.

It is interesting when one considers the laws of the game that a batsman can only be out if the fielding side has appealed. In the days when the laws were drawn up, when playing the game was more important than winning, the umpire was a necessary adjunct as an arbitrator was needed for one or two decisions such as "run out". Presumably, in those days of high moral standards (or were they), a fielder would not appeal for a catch unless there had been a genuine catch. The point is that in most cases the fielder knows better than the umpire whether a catch has been made, whether the ball has crossed the boundary, etc. etc. and therefore if everybody was absolutely trustworthy, it would be better to leave the decision to the fielder. This was achieved by including a law that the fielders, once they had made the catch, let the umpire know by appealing. This avoided the umpire giving the batsman out incorrectly. A bump-ball, where the ball hits the ground immediately before it goes into the fielder's hands, is a good example. The fielder is more likely to know than the umpire what happened in that split second. Of course, after the appeal the umpire is the final arbiter and he makes the decision whether the batsman stays or goes. It may be time to reconsider the laws to exclude appealing and let the umpires make the decision without any interference. This would achieve little however by itself because the aggressive behaviour of the fielders would still occur with whatever consequences on the decisions of the umpire.

Having postulated on umpires in the last paragraph, further consideration suggested that a little research into the history of the game would be appropriate. Teresa Mclean's book, "The Men in White Coats", is particularly informative. So much for the supposition that the game of cricket started as a genteel entertainment for gentlefolk! I discover that cricket was played as early as the seventeenth century and was far from the gentle pastime I had imagined. It was a hard life in those days, even for the aristocracy. If they backed the wrong man or supported the wrong religion, they could soon end up on the end of a noose, and even the death had to be unpleasantly endured whilst the executioners enjoyed themselves with the delights of drawing and quartering and such heinous activities. Many people lived on the breadline or existed beneath it. Life was often unfair, and always rough and ready. It is natural therefore that cricket fitted the times, and it did. Cricket often featured in coroner's reports, and the game was played with such violence that deaths were not uncommon. Indeed, the first umpires were appointed not to administer laws, which were few anyway, but to arbitrate in the disputes between the protagonists and to try to prevent brawling and to steer the game to a peaceful conclusion. Cricket was looked upon as an evil by many because it was inextricably linked with those other evils, drinking and gambling. The matches in the early days were usually arranged and sponsored by publicans for the very good reason that beer which they brewed for special occasions, such as cricket matches or horse races, was exempt from excise duty. The beer was cheap and therefore the events were well attended and much beer was sold.

The publicans often provided the prizes which might be money or items of clothing, or food or drink or other merchandise. It did not seem to matter, because the event provided the opportunity for the poorer element to have a good drink on the cheap, whilst the monied people gambled huge amounts of cash which far exceeded the value of any prizes for the winners. It was normal for several matches to be played on the same day, following each other, and this was possible because the games were different from today and included single wicket matches and other variations which could be completed in a short space of time, thus providing the opportunity for a day of gambling. It was so unusual for gentlemen to play without gambling that one cricket club advertised for gentlemen members by boasting its distinguishing feature, that it played for diversion only.

The sides which took part in the matches usually had patrons, and some of these were the biggest gamblers of all. They were members of the aristocracy or wealthy businessmen of means, and it was normal for them to assemble good sides by employing the best cricketers as employees on their estates, as butlers, coachmen, gamekeepers, etc. They also provided the umpires, and in those rowdy times gave protection to their umpire. Squabbles and disputes were common and many matches failed to finish, as one side declined to continue for one reason or another. It was in the interests of the gamblers to see a match to its conclusion, or alternatively to get it abandoned, depending upon the state of the game and whether they had backed the winning team. When the Duke of Richmond's team played a Mr. Brodrick's side, they drew up a list of rules including that none of the gamesters should query the umpire's decisions on penalty of being ejected from the ground. There was a saving clause which exempted the Duke and Mr. Brodrick! Games often degenerated into pitched battles and fines for riot and battery were commonplace.

Thus, umpires were far from being independent, unbiased arbiters. It was expected of them that they would do their best for their team, otherwise they could find themselves without a job. Even in village cricket, it did not do to upset those on whom you depended for your daily bread or social enjoyment. If you were the village blacksmith, the wrong umpiring decisions could lead to the village baker having his horse shod elsewhere.

The partisanship of umpires was quite openly acknowledged, and at one time it was quite customary to give the umpire of the winning side a share of the prize. In 1771, a Reading newspaper advertised *"a game of cricket for eleven good hats to be played on Tunworth Down on Whit Monday. A hat will be given to the umpire on the winning side."*

There were those sides who were keen to play entirely fairly, but not to the extent that they were prepared to forfeit an equal chance of winning. Thus, there was the case of the village umpire who had given satisfactory service, but it was decided to stand him down in a certain competition as *"being a little too fair, bearing in mind the peculiarities of other umpires in that particular competition."*

One duty the umpires had in the early days was to hold the staff or bat which the batsman had to touch to complete a run. Later the batsman had to place the end of his narrow curved bat into a hole in front of the wickets before the stumper could put the ball into the same hole. This was the origin of the popping crease, or popping hole as it was at that time. The number of mutilated wicket-keeper's hands can be imagined. As they did not wear gloves, it was not a popular position to play. For a long time batsmen could not be thrown out as opposed to run out i.e. the fielders could not throw the wicket down. They had to return the ball to the wicket-keeper for him to place it into the popping hole in order to run out the batsman.

Other peculiarities of the game at that time included the batsman being permitted to obstruct the fielders from catching the ball. Some games allowed for catches to be made, *"clothed or unclothed"*. If you were wearing a hat which many did, you could catch the ball in your hat. A method of dismissal long since gone from our vocabulary was *"nipped out"*. This was simply a variation of caught out, but from a snick or light touch of the ball by the batsman rather than a full-blooded stroke. The specialist close-in fielders of the day stood in the nips rather than at silly point or mid-off.

In turn, underarm daisy-cutter bowling gave way to under-arm lob bowling, then to round-arm, and eventually to over-arm. Each change took place over a period of years, with much opposition to each new method and attempts to outlaw it. Umpires were reluctant to adjudicate as they might be invoking the wrath of their patrons. Also many of the umpires by the nineteenth century were old players and were not happy at the prospect of putting their former colleagues out of work. Eventually the success of each new method promoted itself and was taken on board and the rules amended accordingly. Hambledon, the Hampshire village, which recruited players from all over the county and became omnipotent towards the end of the eighteenth century, was fortunate to have a historian to leave us an insight into cricket of that era. John Nyren writes that when his father started bowling slow left-arm lobs to a length, he was so successful that he bowled 170 balls for only one run. There might have been initial opposition to the new method, but with that sort of success it wasn't likely to be kept out of the arena for very long.

When round-arm bowling was first introduced, the exponents had varying degrees of skill. Even the most skilful bowled a high percentage of wides. It needed a great deal of practice to be able to run up to the wicket and go round the stumps with the arm swinging across the body and land the ball near the wicket. In 1836, there was a single wicket match between the Rev. Pycroft and J.C. Ryle when all 149 runs were scored without the ball once touching the bat! There were 95 byes, 44 wides and 10 no-balls.

Returning to the theme of umpires and their patrons, the Coventry Mercury newspaper report of the 1789 Coventry/Leicester match is revealing. The previous year the match had ended in bloodshed. The paper reports, *"Clarke, who had been declared out on the previous evening by both umpires, made his appearance with his bat at the command of Mr. Needham* (the patron), *who exclaimed 'Clarke keep to your stumps; damn ye Brown* (his umpire) *why do ye not call play?'"*. . . Needham swore that if Mr. Bunbury, the opposition umpire, would not let him go in again, the match should not be played out. It wasn't! This would seem incredible today, but it was all too common then. It probably saved Needham a lot of prospective gambling debts. How often he could repeat such blatant match-saving without being set upon presumably depended on how mob-handed he arrived. The ploy used by Needham was often stymied by a rule for the match that if one side left the field, the match was awarded to the side remaining on the field of play.

By the middle of the nineteenth century, betting on cricket matches had declined considerably. This was due to a number of factors. In 1818, Lord's banned bookies from the ground and presumably other grounds did likewise or later followed suit. Single wicket matches lost their popularity, and these had been easiest for the fixers. In 1835 umpires were forbidden to bet on matches, although this particular move was not very productive in reducing betting by the fixers as they simply saw it as the removal of a powerful force in the betting complex - the best efforts of "fixing" could be undone by the umpire who might be doing a little fixing himself. Clubs gradually became more conscious of their reputations and that they should not be sullied. More professionals and increasing numbers of good players made fixing more difficult and betting more hazardous.

So, had we now turned the corner and reached that utopia whereby cricketers were men of honour and the game was played in the right spirit. Well no, not quite! In 1853, The Times reported a law case, Lane v Barnes. James Lane and his brother John were playing in a match against Westminster school. Barnes, playing for the school, visited the Wellington Tavern during a break for rain and became drunk. When the match restarted, Barnes bowled to John Lane and appealed for lbw. Barnes' brother was umpiring and gave Lane out. Lane disagreed. Angry words were exchanged and Barnes punched Lane on the nose. Lane dared him to repeat the offence, whereupon Barnes seized a bat and brought Lane to the ground with a severe blow to the ankle. Lane was off work for some time and was awarded £60 compensation. This example shows that there could still be problems, but things were improving. To ensure fair play, it was quite common in the north to have four umpires to avoid eccentric individual decisions, or two umpires and a referee to decide on disputes between them. And you thought that the introduction of the third umpire was something new!

In 1884 the laws included a subtle change with regard to umpires. In future umpires were appointed one for each end, not one for each team! Neutrality of umpires was upon us. They, at last, had become a force in their own right - not always to the satisfaction of everybody, of course. At the beginning of the twentieth century, Bob Thoms once gave Gilbert Jessop not out in a match at the Hastings festival though he had been clearly run out by several yards. The bowler complained about the decision and Thoms replied, *"Sixpenny gate, holiday crowd. Can't disappoint 'em. But near thing sir, very near thing."* Umpires' status had improved immeasurably, including sometimes even the necessity to weigh up their duty to the public as opposed to cricketing propriety!

As we head towards the end of the twentieth century, the lot of umpires has become almost unbearable, pilloried and challenged as they are by television replays, slow motion analysis, intimidation and deception by players. There are calls from some quarters for professional umpires - as if that would make a jot of difference. There is little doubt that more and more outside aids will be introduced to try to get accurate decisions, and the powers of the umpires will be eroded. The very nature of their job dictates that they will seldom be loved and are in the unenviable position of receiving no thanks for making 999 correct decisions, but will be unmercifully criticised for one dubious one. I take my hat off to them - at least until they make a decision which I don't like!

5.

TALLY-HO TO THE TWENTIES

SO, HOW DID J.C. fare at the start of the twenties? The answer is exceedingly well. Without any doubt he had become the star of the team, and it has to be acknowledged that it was usually a fairly moderate team, still depending upon amateurs to support the two or three professionals, of whom Braund and Robson were the best. From all accounts Somerset may not have been the best team in the championship but they were certainly one of the happiest. That does not only apply to the amateurs either because Vic Robson confirms that his father enjoyed his cricket.

"1920 saw Sammy Woods appointed secretary (I hope he had a good assistant) *of Somerset bringing that most popular cricketer again in close touch with the team of which he was so long the mainstay."* So reports Wisden. I find it difficult to believe that the ebullient Sammy was ever not in touch with the team, but I suppose he now had an official position. Incidentally, the piece in brackets was not in the Wisden report, that is my addition. I can't believe that Sammy would have spent too long at a desk, doing secretary's work, entertaining the guests with his stories and bonhomie was more in his line. Sammy was known by everyone in Somerset, and he knew a good many of them. He lodged at The George Inn in Taunton for a time, and would stroll around Taunton calling in at the back-parlours (normally reserved for family only) of little shops where he would discuss not only the fortunes of Somerset and other matters of national account, but also little Tommy's toothache and what he might be doing with himself in ten years time when launched into the big world outside.

By the time Sammy became secretary, he had become quite lame from rheumatism in the hip. He attributed this to falling off a camel in Egypt. He told Robertson-Glasgow, who he befriended when he came to Somerset, *"I was in charge of a bunch of those sods, when they stampeded and made for a cactus forest: so off I rolled and fell a bit wrong."*

Sammy was one of those wonderful legends who had a good word to say for everyone. Even his criticisms were spoken or written with a postscript which emphasised the accused's better points to such an extent that the reader or listener remembered the laudatory postscript rather than the original critical comment. He had the gift of making everyone he met feel that little bit better when he departed than before he had met them. That was perhaps understandable with those who worshipped him for his heroic deeds on the field of play. Such mere mortals derive immense pleasure from the slightest contact or acknowledgement from their idols. But Sammy shed his sunshine on everyone, including his equals and betters (if there were any). He usually deflected compliments from his peers by replying graciously with a counter-compliment of equal or greater merit. An example was when he met that Surrey batting legend, little Bobby Abel at the Oval. By this time Bobby was nearly blind, but there would be no difficulty knowing that Sammy was around, from the chatter, even if he had difficulty seeing him. He touched Sammy on the arm and said, *"Oh, Mr. Woods, the times you've nearly knocked my head off out in the middle."* Bobby had been a professional, whilst Sammy was an amateur, hence the formal address. Back came the response, *"Ah, Bobby, but the times you carved me off your whiskers to the boundary."*

Sammy was playing in the match when the great W.G. scored his hundredth century. He would rib the great man unmercifully and told lovely stories about Grace's gamesmanship, but he would hear nothing against him. The Somerset wicket-keeper in that match later said that Grace let only five balls past the bat in the whole innings. A little bit of that wouldn't do any harm today. We can dream up all kinds of ploys to tempt the cricketing public into the grounds, but nothing is guaranteed to succeed like entertaining batting. After the match, the Gloucestershire supporters gave W.G. a complimentary dinner. Again, quoting from Sammy Woods as told to Robertson-Glasgow, *"He drank something of everything, before and during the dinner, and afterwards, he sent for the whisky. You couldn't make the Old Man drunk. His nut was too large. About midnight, some of us thought we might start for home; but the Old Man said to me: 'Shock'ead, get two others, and we'll play rubbers of whist till two in the morning.' So we did."* I can't help thinking that Sammy wouldn't have needed much persuading, and similar stories could be told about Sammy Woods.

One note in Wisden concerning the 1920 season refers to Somerset laments over the number of catches dropped, White being the bowler who suffered most. So it appears, with a decent catching side, J.C. would have had even better figures than the superb sets which placed him in the top few bowlers in the country. I can't really believe that John Daniell, the captain, who was a superb close fielder, would have tolerated a sloppy fielding side, and don't forget that Daniell recruited most of the amateurs himself from the Universities. But someone gave the information to Wisden - perhaps it was Jack White!

White had become so essential to the Somerset side that, even though he was a slow bowler, he often opened the bowling, usually with Ernest Robson. This was not always appreciated by other members of the team, as we shall learn about later.

In the early twenties there is little doubt that Worcestershire were White's rabbits; he repeatedly put them to the sword. Each year they must have hoped that he would be busy with haymaking or the harvest or some other farming necessity. Farmer White was cute enough to sense easy pickings, and whilst I'm sure that he did not choose his matches, he would have been unlikely to miss the Worcester game. In 1920 Somerset beat Worcester by an innings and 155 runs and White claimed 10 wickets for 73 runs.

Later in the year Derbyshire, who were described as the worst of the Counties in that particular year, were beaten by 10 wickets, and Farmer White reaped 12 for 79. Perhaps the best illustrations of White's worth to his team were in the matches which they lost, when White would still have an analysis which most bowlers would not only be proud of but would expect to put them on the winning side. An example is the match against Sussex, where White took 9 wickets for 174, but Somerset were comprehensively beaten. The following week at Bristol, even White buckled to the pressure. Gloucester had been dismissed in their first innings for 22, Robson and White doing the damage. J.C. had the incredible figures of 7 wickets for 10 runs from 9 overs. Gloucester were set 276 to win in their second innings after Somerset had declared, and they got them. White took 1 for 65!

White was 10th in the national bowling averages that year with 138 wickets at an average of 16.05 made at just over two an over. The 1922 Wisden, referring to the previous year, states, *"The mainstay of the Somerset team, as in 1920, was J.C. White. Considering the character of the summer the slow bowler was even better than before, taking 137 wickets in County matches for 15.5 runs each, as against 130 wickets for 14.5. He did not get the support he deserved. Everything depended upon White and although he had days of wonderful success, taking on one occasion all 10 wickets in one innings, it is not surprising that the burden laid upon him proved too great. Still, he had a great season, and he had the honour of being picked for the Test match at Leeds. It struck one that, without any loss of length or any change in his puzzling flight, he bowled with more spin than in previous years."*

The game where he took all ten wickets in an innings was, as you might suspect, against hapless Worcestershire. For the record, again opening the bowling with Robson, he took 10 wickets for 76 runs in 42.2overs, Oh, incidentally, he took a further five wickets in the second innings.

1921 was a vintage year for White and it is not intended to bore you with his repeated successes, many times he exceeded 10 wickets in a match. Once more, however, his worth is demonstrated to me by his performances in matches which the team lost. A further example was against Gloucestershire in May. The latter won the match by 110 runs, and yet White's match analysis was 13 wickets for 78 runs! He was a fairly taciturn character but he must sometimes have harboured inner thoughts on the inadequacies of his companions.

Never noted for his batting, least not since his schooldays, White was starting to develop his all-rounder skills, which were to peak at the end of the decade. He had his highest score for the County at Derby where he batted at No. 5 and reached 80, to add to the 13 wickets which he had taken. A terse Wisden comment, *"White clearly won the match for Somerset."*

It was in 1921 that Farmer White played his first game for his country. He had played in representative games previously, notably for the Gentlemen, but at the age of 30 he at last was chosen for England, and who against, none other than the Australians. Thirty might seem a late age to commence a Test career when judged by today's standards, but in those days cricketers' careers often took them into their forties and even fifties. Dear Ernest Robson was still opening the bowling for Somerset, and often very successfully, and he had reached his half-century that very year. Consequently the age a cricketer was invited into the top level was much later than would be the case now. Without doubt there was also a policy that newcomers should get some years of experience under their belts before they could be considered to be fit to play with the best. Australia would say today that England still retains a very conservative approach to blooding youngsters, but a current dearth of talent of any age in England probably means that the door is open to anyone showing the necessary skills.

It will not have escaped cricketing buffs that one of the Test selectors in 1921 was none other than John Daniell, the Somerset captain. It has to be assumed that this did not disadvantage Jack White when the team was being picked for the third Test. England had been whitewashed 5-0 the previous year in Australia. In the five matches, Australia had scored nearly 600 runs more than England for the loss of 27 fewer wickets, and their average score per wicket was forty-six to England's twenty-seven. The games had not taken place without some "aggravation", notably in criticisms of umpiring decisions (nothing is new) and crowd barracking of the England players. This latter was attributed to the fact that certain of the English players (Rockley Wilson and Percy Fender in particular) were playing the role of part-time journalists and exception was taken to some of the reports which they sent to England.

The current administration have rules and regulations to guard against this type of trouble, but it still manifests itself and keeps the Press and the public, not to mention the administrators, active for many a day. There is little doubt that the news media, at least, regard the events surrounding major sporting events to be of just as much interest as the event itself. Writing a book teaches you why. All matches are basically the same even though they have their differences, and to some that is boring. Statistics can certainly be, except to a few. So a little human content in the story, be it congratulatory praise or malicious gossip, helps considerably to spice up the report. Unfortunately, it has reached the point where some unscrupulous hacks fabricate stories without any foundation. This causes distress to those concerned, but also means that the public starts to doubt all stories and they lose their meaning.

Jack White's introduction to the Test match stage at Leeds was due as much to dire necessity on behalf of the selectors as to his County performances, brilliant as these were. Following the 5-0 whitewash in Australia, England had been comprehensively defeated at Nottingham in two days and at Lord's in two days and a half. In the series England were to field no less than thirty different men. It was not the ideal introduction; England were desperate for immediate results. As has been said many times since, it is most unfair to judge a player on one match only. Even the proven and established players can't perform to their very best on every occasion.

In the event, J.C. bowled quite creditably, taking 3 wickets for 107 off 37 overs. Not exactly vintage White, but it wasn't bad. But the point was that England again lost, taking their sequence of losses to eight. The selectors made further changes for the following Test and White found himself back on the sidelines, where he would remain for a further seven years. Not that he did not have the opportunity in that period but his farming made him miss at least one tour, and apparently he made himself unavailable for Gilligan's team in 1924.

Returning to the 1921 series, England fared rather better in the last two Tests, drawing both; but there were those who said that Australia, having won the rubber, were not too concerned. Armstrong, the Australian captain, was past forty and weighed seventeen stone and was likened to an Australian W.G. Grace, both in size and ability. He was an astute captain but little was required of him in that capacity in 1921 as the Australian strike bowlers Gregory and McDonald, backed up by Arthur Mailey, were much too good for England. Armstrong was a man of few words but when he did speak he meant it and people were inclined to listen - as they do when a man weighs seventeen stone.

The tour was soured by one or two petty squabbles between the autocratic M.C.C. hierarchy and the Australians. Reasonably, Armstrong demanded a rest day for his players before each Test. Those at Lord's liked making the rules and appeared to resent such intrusion into their birthright. Later, Armstrong requested that drinks should be served to his players in the dressing-room at Lord's, and this was contested by the Secretary of M.C.C., who considered that the bar was the only place where such activity was justified. On the last day of the Oval Test, Armstrong retired to the outfield and picked up a newspaper which had blown across the ground, which he read between overs. He later made an ill-advised joke of the incident by stating that he was reading the paper to find out who they were playing! It is thought that his actions on the last day were a protest against the England custom of the time of restricting Test matches to three days. As the first three games had been won well within this timescale, and there was provision for the fifth and last game to continue to a conclusion had the series depended upon it, his stance was not appreciated.

After 1921 there were no Test matches at home for three years. F. T. Mann was captain of a tour to South Africa in 1922/23 but J.C. White did not make the trip.

In 1921 White once more headed the Somerset bowling with 137 wickets at 15.56. Robson, at the ripe old age of 50 was second in the County averages with 81 wickets at 25.17. In the national table, White had risen to 5th with 143 first-class wickets at an average of 17.07.

1921 also saw the retirement of Len Braund. At the turn of the century he had been one of the contenders for the title of best all-rounder in the world. Not only had he been a prolific and classic batsman and a highly successful bowler, but he had also been in the highest grade of fielders and close-in catchers. He was an extremely wise judge of cricket and knew the strengths and weaknesses of all his opponents and how to exploit that knowledge. In later years he had the misfortune of having to have both of his legs amputated, but he coped admirably with this tragedy. Why does life so often treat our heroes so abominably. Tom Young and George Hunt joined Somerset as new professionals.

Wisden comments for the 1922 season included, *"J.C. White was the dominating figure in the Somerset XI. The heavy grounds did not help him, but he was even more successful than in 1921. In some matches he did great things."* The details are almost a repeat of the previous year. Once more he "did" Worcestershire, this time taking 14 wickets for 84 runs. But Worcestershire did not lose this game - no, it rained with their last pair at the wicket and still needing 138 to make Somerset bat again. Once more there were the examples of matches lost in spite of superb bowling performances by White, notably 11 wickets against Kent.

In 1922 White was 10th in the first-class averages with 146 victims at an average of 15.63. Somerset were fortunate that year that the amateur J.C.W. MacBryan was more regularly available and he led the batting averages for the County with 1457 runs at an average of 34. Restricted availability of their best amateur batsmen had been Somerset's main problem for many years.

It was in this year that the first wireless commentary took place on a cricket match, and it was in New South Wales that the event occurred. Prior to that, your only alternatives were to be at the match or read about it some time later.

1924 Wisden (for the 1923 season) reads, *"Somerset won nine (against six in 1922) but lost eleven. J.C. White, one of the very best amateur bowlers, was just the same bowler as in 1922 - immaculate in length and untiring. His record was almost a repetition of what it had been the year before - 141 wickets as against 146 and within a fraction of the same average. For a great part of the season he received no real help except from Bridges. . . (but later in the season Robertson-Glasgow was a great strength)."*

In the 1923 summer, J.C. took 10 wickets or more against Gloucestershire, Hampshire, Warwickshire and, of course, Worcestershire (twice). On the second occasion, against the latter, the game was over in less than two days. He also took six wickets against the touring West Indians at Weston-super-mare. This was before their tours were given Test match status.

J.C. rose to be 3rd in the national averages for his bowling with 148 wickets at an average of 15.50, and his season was enhanced with a hat-trick against Middlesex at Lord's, the headquarters of cricket. His batting still left a deal to be desired, his average being only 15.25 with a top score of 60.

This was a year when Somerset should have achieved more success; MacBryan had been Somerset's most reliable batsman since the war and Lyon, another former Cambridge man, had matured and become a good forcing batsman. Respectively, they had 1500 runs at an average of 38, and 1100 runs at an average of 33.

Perhaps the game of the year was Somerset v Surrey at Bath in early May. It was a game full of memories and performances which would be told to small boys on their fathers' knees for many years to come. It was also a game which swung violently in favour of one side against the other. In writing at some length about this match, it gives us the opportunity to pay tribute to the greatest of all England's batsmen - Jack Hobbs. Who says so? Well, Sir Donald Bradman, to start with.

At that time only two cricketers had scored a hundred hundreds, W.G. Grace and Tom Hayward. Jack Hobbs was 41 years of age, a comparative youngster as far as cricket was concerned in those days. He needed one more "ton" to reach his century, and this was the match he chose. In the following two years, he would overtake both of his predecessors, and it would be against Somerset in 1925 that he would exceed Grace's record of 126 centuries. When he completed the hundredth century, he had amassed (and there is probably no better word to describe it) 34,534 runs. The amazing fact is that in the following eleven years to his eventual retirement, he added a further 27,000 runs to his total and 97 more centuries. Who said cricketers were over the top at forty? He certainly didn't seem to need his Phyllosan. Incidentally, he missed four years cricket due to the First World War.

The Somerset v Surrey match was scheduled to start on the Saturday, but wet weather meant that three overs only were bowled on that first day, and they were three maidens. The opening bowlers were Ernest Robson and Jack White.

On the Monday the same duos opened again, and without a run on the board Robson, in his 52nd year, had spoiled any plans that Hobbs had for celebrating his hundred hundreds that particular day. Daniell had brought off one of the brilliant catches for which he was noted, but this time at cover-point rather than closer in at silly-point, his more usual position. I presume his standing some thirty yards further back was in deference to the man who was batting. And do you recall what Ernest Robson had said to his son Victor, *"I always felt you had some chance against Jack Hobbs early in his innings."* He had added, *"Let him get started and you would live to regret it."* Keep that in mind until a little later.

Robson and J.C. bowled magnificently, and Surrey struggled for nigh on three hours before they were all out for 91. Of that total Ducat had made 52 not out! White had 4 wickets for 27 runs in 30.3 overs, economy at its best; and the quinquagenerian took 6 wickets for 59 off 33 overs. Not bad, for an old 'un. Surrey had been routed and Somerset had the initiative. They batted spiritedly but everyone seemed to get out just when they seemed set, and the result was a total of 140. Not too bad when one considered the Surrey score.

Early in Surrey's second innings, White caught Sandham plumb in front of his stumps, but by the end of play for the day Surrey had reduced the deficit by half. On the resumption of play on the Tuesday, Surrey lost Ducat, their only hero in the first innings, run out. Not heeding the warning, a short time later, Shepherd was also run out. Percy Fender joined Hobbs, who was again not starting well and who again started for an ill-judged run. Fender sternly sent him back, and but for a blunder in the field by MacBryan, he must have been run out. Back come those words, *"Let him get started and you will live to regret it."* Fender went and Surrey were still behind the Somerset total with four wickets already down. It looked good for Somerset and Jack Hobbs' desired century appeared an extremely remote possibility.

The scene then changed, Hobbs found a willing partner in Hitch and the score started to mount, slowly at first before breaking into a gallop. Hobbs' second fifty came in only a touch over the hour and Surrey soon declared. The purpose of the story is now complete, to celebrate Jack Hobbs' hundred hundreds, but the game continued to an exciting conclusion, Surrey eventually being the unlikely winners by 10 runs in uncertain light in play sensibly extended to find a winner.

It is interesting to compare the compositions of the two teams. Surrey comprised ten professionals led by their only amateur, Percy Fender.

Somerset fielded four professionals, rather more than normal, and had seven amateurs.

We will now skip a couple of years, and we find ourselves in August 1925. Jack Hobbs is back in Somerset with the Surrey team, though this time the venue is Taunton as opposed to Bath. There are some significant changes in the personnel involved. Unfortunately Ernest Robson is no longer with us, having retired from playing. He was denied his debut as an umpire and died in Bristol Infirmary. John Daniell is also absent, having severely strained a leg whilst scoring centuries in both innings, 174 not out and 108, against Essex some weeks earlier. Not bad for a man of 46. A notable appearance in the Surrey team is that of D.R. Jardine, later to captain England in the Bodyline series.

It was 20th July when Hobbs scored his 125th century, leaving him one short of the Grace record, and since that time a posse of cricket reporters had followed him everywhere, waiting for the kill. He had kept them waiting, having failed to see the act through against Sussex, Kent, Gloucestershire and Nottinghamshire, where a young newcomer called Larwood had him caught for one. On the 15th August the circus arrived at Taunton, wearied but ever hopeful and fearful to miss the big moment. The secretary of Somerset was delighted to see the large crowd but apprehensive when the motion-picture people started to clamber onto the tin roof of the old pavilion.

All were kept waiting, as Somerset won the toss and elected to bat first. It was a sorry innings, and Robertson-Glasgow, who was playing in the game, stated that, *"we batted as if the world was waiting for something better."* Which, of course, it was. But what a lovely description. Somerset made 167; and at 4.00pm Hobbs and his faithful sidekick, Sandham, approached the crease to much cheering and satisfaction. It was generally agreed that most of those present, and most were Somerset supporters, wanted Hobbs to succeed. Today, with more partisan crowds, I wonder whether that would be the case. Certainly the press wanted him to succeed, the excitement was growing a bit thin. Hobbs started uncertainly and he carried on in the same vein - his timing was not up to scratch - and he fought his way onwards, his many years of experience keeping him afloat. By close of play he had reached 91, sheer doggedness had got him there. It is strange that such an innings gives less satisfaction than one of consummate ease and skill and beauty, because the effort in reaching the goal must necessarily be much greater and more problems have been overcome, even if some are of your own making. One man, particularly, had been instrumental in keeping him on target, and that was D.J. Knight, who had replaced Sandham when the latter was caught. Hobbs called him for a very quick single, and Knight called "No", but Hobbs was on his way. Quickly Knight went for what he knew was the impossible, and just managed to pass Hobbs before the wickets were downed - a sacrifice if ever there was.

Jack Hobbs spent a quiet weekend, and kept to himself much of the time at his hotel, though he was pursued to some extent by the photographers. He attended church on the Sunday morning, and I expect he made sure that he avoided any convivial sessions with Sammy Woods. On Monday, play started late as the Somerset groundstaff ushered a half-mile long queue into the ground, all intent on seeing the climax (or witnessing the calamity). The Somerset management beamed with satisfaction at the sight of so many bottoms on seats.

There was no way that the Somerset bowlers were going to present Hobbs with his century. They were intent on nailing him so that they could tell the story to their friends and family ad nauseam thereafter. Three singles took Hobbs to 94, and bless me if Robertson-Glasgow didn't bowl a no-ball. That was an opportunity which Hobbs did not disparage and it went to the boundary like a rocket. 98 - a short wait and two more singles and the ordeal was over. The crowd went bananas and everyone wanted to shake Jack Hobbs by the hand. Percy Fender came out onto the pitch with a glass which contained a liquid, the exact identity of which was not revealed. There was much speculation, as can be imagined, but later Jack Hobbs maintained that it contained only ginger ale. What an opportunity he and the advertisers missed. Handled in the right manner, somebody's sales could have been doubled as the public purchased the magic elixir which had brought the hero to his success. Three overs and one run later Hobbs was out, even he must have found continued concentration impossible.

Taunton had witnessed the making of a little piece of history, and at the time could not contemplate that a second helping was just around the corner. It was J.C.W. MacBryan, that extremely good Somerset batsman, who made the sequel possible. In Somerset's second innings, he played one of his finest, to score a century in two and a quarter hours. It was the foundation of a Somerset total of 374. This meant that Surrey required 183 runs to win.

Was it possible? Surely not. No, he couldn't, could he?

Out came Hobbs and Sandham once more. This time it was a

different Jack Hobbs; it was the batsman that everyone had read about so often, the scourge of bowlers, the imperious stroke-maker, the English flag-bearer on the field of combat. All his worries of the first innings were brushed aside and his timing was sweetness itself, as balls were dispatched to the boundary rails. If Sandham held himself in check, it was not noticeable, but Hobbs went to his hundred, Grace's record overtaken, and Surrey had won.

After the game, Hobbs was persuaded to appear on the pavilion balcony, where he congratulated the groundsman, Harry Fernie, on a good wicket, and stated that if the record could not be achieved at the Oval, there was no better place than Taunton. A member of the press asked him of his intentions with regard to the bat with which he had achieved the record and whether he might give it to the British Museum, for posterity. Hobbs replied that he had not decided, but that he had already been offered a hundred guineas for it. As it happened, and not widely known, he used two bats on that day. Now that today would go down to brilliant marketing; he could give one to posterity and sell the other and make a few bob. No such grasping notions in Jack Hobbs' head, the bat eventually went to the Daily News "Wireless for Hospitals Fund." Which bat?

Hobbs was the celebrity of the moment, and in one B.B.C. interview told a nice story at the expense of the previous record holder. W.G. Grace was famous for wanting to be at the centre of the action, and on this particular day he had bowled unsuccessfully for a very long time. Most members of his team would have been afraid to comment, but W.L. Murdoch approached the doctor and diplomatically suggested that it was about time that he had a change. *"Good idea Bill"* came the response, *"I'll try the other end!"* For the record, the other story which he told concerned Tom Hayward. He was batting one day with Hobbs, when a new bowler was introduced to the attack. Hayward cracked him for 14 off his first over. At the end of the over Hobbs said to Hayward that he thought the bowler was throwing. *"Of course he is,"* said Hayward. *"Don't say anything or they will take him off."*

A final word on the Hobbs match; we haven't mentioned J.C. White. Was he playing? Oh yes, very much so, but this was Hobbs' match and with the possible exception of MacBryan's century, nothing which Somerset could do would change that fact. White was as economical as ever and bowled 43 overs for one wicket and 85 runs. It was noticeable to all concerned that Jack Hobbs treated Jack White with a great deal of caution and sought his runs elsewhere. The same story would apply to most of the country's top batsmen. They had come to learn that White was a bowler to treat with respect, runs came much more easily from other sources and with much less risk to boot. Hendren said that Hobbs, Hammond, and the other top right-handers treated White with kid gloves, only the left-handed Woolley seemed prepared to have a go at J.C. and he did so quite successfully on more than one occasion. It isn't surprising really, every top-notch batsman prefers the ball coming in to him rather than the one leaving him.

Returning to 1924, Jack White had yet another superb season, he bowled 980.4 overs for 1986 runs, and took 135 wickets at the outstanding average of only 14.34. He also had an improved year with the bat and scored 595 runs at an average of 22.03. Somerset also had a good year and recorded nine wins against seven losses with eight games being drawn. In the last match of the season, they defeated Worcestershire by 10 wickets and J.C. had 3 for 54 from 30 overs in the first innings, and 8 for 44 from 20 overs in the second innings. He also scored 34 runs. Incidentally, the other two wickets which fell in the Worcestershire second innings were run-outs!

The year was notable for two other matters. Firstly, it was Ernest Robson's swan-song. After the yeoman service he had given for so many years he was to hang up his boots and bat, and don the white coat of the umpiring fraternity. Unfortunately, an illness and early death deprived him and cricket followers of that pleasure. It is shear speculation, but I imagine he would have been one of the most impartial umpires on the circuit. There would have been a huge sympathy for the batsman caught plumb in front before he had scored, or for the perspiring bowler who had sweated all day without success, but the decision he would give would be the correct one. If you can't play fairly, you shouldn't play at all, would have been one of the maxims by which Ernest lived. No doubt there were various functions arranged to provide him with a benefit; the County permitted him a competition at their match with the South African tourists. Entrants had to estimate the number of people who would attend the match, the prize being an A.J.S. motor-cycle valued at £52. The proceeds were £280, just about £10 per year for the years he had played for Somerset.

The amateur, M.D. Lyon, had become one of Somerset's most reliable batsmen and an excellent wicket-keeper, and the County had high hopes of him for many years to come. But 1924 saw those hopes severely dashed. Lyon was to become a well-known barrister, and was good enough at cricket to be on the edge of selection for his country, but he was no shrinking violet, and considered himself badly done by when he was not chosen for the first Test-match of that year against the South Africans, missing out to a young newcomer from the North, one George Duckworth. Poor Duckworth also missed out, as it rained in Manchester throughout the period allocated for the Test and there was no play, and it would be a further four years before he would receive his second invitation.

Lyon had played in the Gentlemen v Players match, but had injured his hand early in the game, and had not been able therefore to demonstrate his wicket-keeping prowess. In apparent pique, he wrote to the M.C.C. after hearing that he had not been selected for the Test, and complained that amateurs were being treated badly!!! There was an exchange of letters, which Lyon later had printed in the Daily Express. In one letter, he wrote, *"Cricket is losing its hold on the people, because with a few exceptions the game as played by the professionals is a dull and wearisome business - perhaps inevitably so."* Fighting talk, not likely to endear him to the professionals. The situation turned sour for Somerset because one of the three Test selectors was none other than John Daniell, the Somerset captain. Daniell informed Lyon that he had actually voted for him, but he had been out-voted by the other two, one of whom was H.D.G. Leveson-Gower.

At the end of the Summer, when the touring side to go to South Africa was being selected, Lyon received a wire from the Honourable Lionel Tennyson, who was to lead the side, as follows: *"To M. D. Lyon:- Shrimp Leveson-Gower, chairman of the selectors for the side to go to South Africa, asks me to wire you, to ask if you would go on trip there, starting middle of October, if asked. Please wire me reply. Lionel Tennyson."*

Back went the reply from Lyon, totally unimpressed by this sop. *"To L. Tennyson:- Very sorry, impossible. Ask me again in twenty years time. Are you sure that shrimps make good mothers? Lyon."*

Mr. Lyon had received a hurt from which he never fully recovered, and Somerset C.C.C. suffered also because he immediately informed them that he would be available only very infrequently in the future. M.D. Lyon's *annus horribilis* was completed by a terse statement in the press at the end of the year informing the public at large that his engagement to a certain lady, announced earlier in the year, had been broken off.

The Somerset Gazette in April 1925 assessed the prospects for the County side in the forthcoming season. It deduced that they were not too good, particularly in respect of the batting. M.D. Lyon, T.C. Lowry, and probably MacBryan would be unavailable - the heart of the batting of the previous year. The bowling led by White, Bridges, and Greswell should be reasonable; but still there were only two professionals, Young and Hunt. True, there were three professionals in the course of qualifying for the County, including Lee, the brother of the Middlesex player, but Somerset were still very reliant on their amateurs. On the social side there was a fillip as the Somerset Stragglers, who shared the County ground, were constructing an enclosure which was to be lavishly fitted out and which would boost the inner man.

The season started in the same vein as many before. Headlines in the Gazette were *"Somerset beaten at Lord's"*, and the sub-heading stated *"Fine bowling by White"*. He took 6 wickets for 43 in 25 overs, including three wickets in four balls, which reduced the home team from the reasonable 106 for 3 to the very moderate 124 for 9. But all to no avail, Somerset were beaten. Then Kent thrashed Somerset, including White who took only one wicket for over a hundred runs. Woolley scored 215 and Kent declared at 548, far too many for Somerset. Lancashire were next. Somerset made 74 in their first innings and 73 in the second. Lancashire totalled 130, and White had 5 for 67, then took the only wicket to fall as Lancashire knocked off the required 18 runs. Oh dear!

Somerset had to wait until their fifth match at the end of May before they achieved their first win. And who obliged? Yes, good old Worcestershire. White had his usual field-day and recorded 5 for 19 off 18 overs in their first innings and followed it with 6 for 42 off 20 overs in the second innings. I expect, if there had been one, he would have been declared man of the match!

On the local scene in Taunton, the County Gazette, perhaps in desperation to produce more home-grown talent, advertised that the worthy Paper would be presenting a bat each week for the best performance in local cricket. What is more, the bats would be no less than the Jack Hobbs "Force" bats of national renown. And I thought Jack knew nothing of promoting his interests. Speaking once more of that great man has reminded me that something strange, at least to me, happened after the Hobbs' record 127th century. Scorecards of the big occasion, printed on silk, were marketed (lovely word) from the Taunton ground. Good idea; but who marketed them - Harry Fernie - the groundsman! I would love to know the background to that. Was it in his contract? Couldn't the County administration be bothered with it? I like to think, probably erroneously (but maybe not), that Sammy Woods had something to do with it, or should I say that Sammy had nothing to do with it. I can just imagine Harry putting the idea to Sammy, as secretary of the County, and Sammy complimenting him and telling him, *"Wonderful idea, my dear. Your idea - your gain."* I don't know whether Harry made any money out of it, but I hope he did. He deserved it. Again I don't know, but I am willing to bet that Tony Stedall has one of the silks in the County Cricket Museum.

Jack White's bowling average for that year was 121 wickets from 1023 overs for 2001 runs (less than two an over) at an average of 16.53. His batting average was almost twenty. He was getting the hang of that part of the game, but it would be another couple of years before he could consider himself an all-rounder.

In researching for information on J.C. and his contemporaries in the back numbers of the Somerset Gazette, I was struck by the frequency of meetings of the County branch of the Agricultural Workers' Union. In 1925 they were not happy with working a 52-hour week in the winter. They seemed to know that it was unavoidable in the summer. It is obvious that they have been trying to squeeze a little more out of the farmers for many a long year. I would not suggest that Jack White had anything to do with such negotiations, I am sure that he did not, but the stubborn resistance of the farmers to anything which would threaten their livelihood seems to be reflected in the way that J.C. played his cricket. He regarded runs as a rare commodity, not to be given away lightly. If the runs were looked after, the wickets would follow, because the batsman with whom he was doing business at the other end of the pitch was greedy to have more runs, and would start taking risks to get his hands on them. Some bowlers were happy to buy their wickets by tossing out a little seed-corn to give the batsman a few runs and to encourage him to take the bait, but J.C. did not often take this course of action. It was anathema to his beliefs to give away runs, whatever the circumstances. He preferred to bowl every ball as perfectly as he could and to wait. He never tired.

In the county north of Somerset, another slow left-armer was having a good season. Charlie Parker of Gloucestershire made the headlines, not for the first time, when he pulverised Essex with match figures of 17 for 56. The previous year he had the almost unique experience of taking two hat-tricks in one game, when Middlesex were the unfortunate victims. By 1925, Parker was 43 years old but he was still bowling well enough to be in the running for representing his country. He had done so on only one occasion, in 1921, and there were many who considered it a gross miscarriage of justice that he had not been picked on more occasions. In 1926, he was included in the twelve for two Tests, but each time became 12th man. On one of the occasions the wicket was exactly to his liking, and Maurice Tate thought it unforgivable that Parker was not chosen. Some said that he could be an argumentative customer and that had not endeared him to the selectors. Also, he was unfortunate to be on the scene at about the same time as Wilfred Rhodes, but there can't be many bowlers with a record like Parker's who have managed only one appearance for their Country. He was no flash in the pan either, as we shall see when we compare Jack White with the other great slow left-arm bowlers of the period.

6.

SOMERSET AND ARGENTINA

1926 IN SOMERSET was not very different from other years, although mention should be made of the advent to the team of E.F. Longrigg, erstwhile captain of Rugby School, and without doubt a left-hand bat of some promise. He was to serve Somerset for some years and eventually took over the captaincy. J.C. White again headed the county bowling averages with 131 wickets from 1351 overs for 2550 runs at an average of 19.45.

On the international scene, it was a year which England had awaited with some anxiety, another opportunity to rest the Ashes from the foe who had retained them for far too long. Since the Great War England had submitted to the Australians on no less than twelve occasions and had only one victory on the credit side. Three series had come and gone - gone to the Australians. But it was more than that; the politicians needed a victory. A land fit for heroes to live in had been promised to those who had survived the holocaust, but that was now a fading dream and in May the unrest had spiralled into the General Strike. Britons needed something to cheer, something to raise their morale and to replace some of their lost pride.

The first four matches of the five-match series were all drawn with England overall having the better of it. Carr of Nottinghamshire was the captain and, after the first match was largely lost to rain, he was loudly applauded for the second match, but he was criticised for putting the Australians in after winning the toss for the third match. Just before the commencement of the fourth game, Carr had the misfortune to go down with tonsilitis and Jack Hobbs deputised as captain. However, he was a professional and at that time it would have been frightfully infra dig to have a pro. as captain on a regular basis. So, we came to the fifth and last Test. A.P.F. Chapman had become the darling of the cricketing public. Although totally inexperienced as a captain, he was a swashbuckling batsman in whom the crowds delighted. The selectors made their choice. Carr was out and Chapman was in.

Also the selectors did what England selectors have often done, not always without success. They chose Wilfred Rhodes, at 49, to resurrect his international career. These decisions were not universally acclaimed, particularly Chapman as captain. He might have been the idol of the public, but the cricketing intelligentsia were much less certain. The leader in the Daily Express queried the reasons for not selecting Hobbs or Rhodes, for example, as captain, and reminded the selectors that the Spanish Armada in 1588 had several experienced admirals in its ranks, but the King of Spain had chosen an amateur, the Duke of Medina Sidonia to be in command - with fatal results. Maurice Tate, who played in all the matches in the series, didn't seem too concerned about the change of captaincy. In his autobiography, he dealt with it in one brief sentence, *"A new captain, A.P.F. Chapman, was appointed."*

The match was scheduled to continue to the finish, but this did not lead to the tedium of slow batting which some feared and 340 runs were scored and 14 wickets taken on the first day. There was not much in it at the end of the first innings, but Hobbs and Sutcliffe then had one of their best days and put on 172 for the first wicket. England amassed 436 and, largely due to Larwood and Rhodes, Australia were dismissed for 126 and England had won by 289 runs. The Daily Telegraph editorial reported that, as Mailey's wickets were spreadeagled, tremendous cheering broke out all round the ground. In the stands, erstwhile grave parsons sacrificed their hats, men hugged each other and danced madly and women grew hysterical. Retired (and usually retiring) military men leapt the barriers and scampered gamely for the pavilion. The Morning Post had erected a giant score-board outside their office in Aldwych and huge crowds had watched throughout the day. Just before six o'clock, the board announced that victory had been gained. All along the Strand and throughout London the news spread like wildfire and resulted in loud and spontaneous cheering. Later, the rest of the country celebrated likewise. Percy Chapman was a hero, the best thing before sliced bread. Fickle sports editors applauded him. What was that about the Spanish Armada? All was well in the world, at least it was in the English cricketing world. The cricketing public licked its lips, Chapman was only 25, think of the things to come, and on this occasion they did.

That winter an M.C.C. party toured South America. Originally the intention had been to visit Argentina only, where cricket was passionately followed, British expatriates having introduced it in the nineteenth century. Cricket was also played in Uruguay, Chile and Peru, and the tour was extended to commence with a game in Montevideo, followed by the games in Argentina, and ending with a crossing of the Andes to show the flag in Valparaiso and Lima, before returning home via the Panama Canal.

The team was totally comprised of amateurs, of varying age and skills, and included one future Prime Minister, Lord Dunglass, who was to become Sir Alec Douglas Home. Plum Warner, at the age of 53, was the captain. At the other end of the scale were three or four in their early twenties, including a fast-maturing Gubby Allen. There were four serving soldiers and three County captains, Guy Jackson of Derbyshire, Maurice Jewell of Worcestershire, and Jack White (see later) of Somerset. White, Allen, and Jameson of Hampshire were expected to do the work. J.C. was now 35 years of age and in his prime. As E.W. Swanton wrote, *"It approximated to a strong Free Forester side such as might at that time have given a good game at Oxford or Cambridge. The point was, it was just about adequate for its purpose on the field and no doubt even better equipped off it."*

The party sailed on the S.S. Andes, and Jack White made his mark in the very first game, which was played at Montevideo on Christmas Eve and Christmas Day. He bowled unchanged throughout the innings and took 7 for 27 as Montevideo struggled to a total of 64. They improved slightly in their second innings to reach 97, but M.C.C. were the winners by an innings and 204 runs. Too much Xmas pudding for the home side no doubt.

The "serious" matches were to be three "Tests" against Argentina. Suffice it to say, rain ended the first game before M.C.C. were half-way through their first innings. M.C.C. won the second game, but a thunderstorm made the pitch quite unplayable in the third game and Argentina squared the series. At short notice a fourth match was arranged at Belgrano (a name to be remembered in a rather different context many years later), to determine the victors. Argentina scored 271 in their first innings and some lively batting by the tail took the M.C.C. reply to 384, at which point, Warner declared. It was a hopeful declaration as only two hours play were left, but J.C. weighed in with 5 wickets for 25 runs and Argentina were all out for 101, five minutes before the close, and M.C.C. had won by an innings. Jack White had played a major part in all the matches.

It was Gubby Allen's only experience of Warner as a captain, but he was highly impressed, particularly with the way that he summed up each opposing player's strengths and weaknesses after an over or two for the benefit of his bowlers.

In going to South America, there must have been thoughts of having to rough it a little, particularly when going up country, but the tourists were treated to exemplary hospitality everywhere and when they did go up country, they lived in a luxurious train with marble baths and sitting rooms which had been built for the Prince of Wales' tour a few years earlier. The tourists, with the possible exception of Lord Home, who suffered with a grumbling appendix which kept him out of several matches and eventually put him into hospital, enjoyed a wonderful holiday.

Jack White was renowned in Somerset almost as much for his poker skills as for his bowling, and the long rail journeys gave him ample opportunity to try out some of his fellow-passengers. As the Andes were crossed their attentions were divided between the magnificent countryside, including Mount Aconcagua, the highest mountain in the Andes, and their dealt hands. Twice Jack White sat comfortably with full houses, aces high, and twice Tommy Jameson nailed him with royal straight flushes. In mock disgust J.C. threw the pack of cards out of the window.

White seems to have been a bad influence on his colleagues regarding gambling, because he was also the author of an infallible system to beat the roulette wheel, and recruited a number of the others to a syndicate with that aim in mind. As with most of such systems, early success was followed by the day when it all went wrong and they lost the lot. Gubby Allen remembered being sent off to inform Lord Home of his misfortune, as he lay in his hospital bed.

J.C. was normally fairly reserved, but all reports put him down as a good tourist. He could enjoy a joke whether giving it or taking it; and sometimes the victims of a practical joke were quite surprised to find that the identity of the perpetrator was a certain J.C. White. His knowledge of country life allowed him to contribute to discussions with their hosts in areas where many of his urban colleagues were ignorant, or at least limited. Discourse on hunting, racing, farming were all very much in his domain. He had a habit of calling people "cock". I am not sure that that would have gone down well on a tour such as that to the Argentine, so perhaps he had the ability to vary his vocabulary according to the circumstances. On the tour to South America, it was reported that he spent much of his time laughing, even when the less able fielders dropped catches off his bowling. There was one particular gentleman who never caught anything. White would turn away and say, *"Tell me when he has dropped it"*. The young Gubby Allen could not display the same lack of concern when catches were dropped off his bowling. What Gubby did not realise was that J.C. would also have had a different attitude had the misdemeanour occurred in a match that mattered. The South American tour was rated only a fun affair to J.C.

Two items of curiosity value bring the South American interlude to a close. The first occurred in Valparaiso in Chile where play was interrupted by an earth tremor. Gubby Allen must have thought that there had been divine intervention on his side when the bails were to be seen lying on the ground in spite of the fact that the ball he bowled was at least a foot outside the off-stump. A more interesting incident occurred in Argentina. H.W. Marshal trod on his wicket when playing a ball from Jack White. He had almost reached the pavilion when he about-turned and returned to the crease to appeal to the bowler's umpire that he was not out. That umpire had been unsighted, so Marshal then appealed to the square-leg umpire, who gave him not out on the grounds that he had completed his stroke when he broke the wicket. Now that would have been a good one for slow-motion replays.

Whilst Jack White was sunning himself in January 1927 in South America, Somerset County Cricket Club was holding its A.G.M. at Bath. J.C. was proposed and unanimously elected to the post of Captain for the forthcoming season in succession to John Daniell, who had expressed a desire to relinquish the post, though it was hoped that he might still assist with the bat when required. Incredibly, the financial position was reported as very satisfactory, and credit for that was accorded to Mr. Davey, the Secretary. The main income was the members' subscriptions and Mr. Davey had apparently been very active in drumming up support in that direction. County membership had risen in three years from 1000 to 4000, and a balance of £1700 was reported. The gate receipts, whilst being very welcome, were considered unreliable. The total income for the year had been £3000, and Somerset's share of the Test matches profits was £1100. It illustrates the Counties' dependency on Test match takings even in those days.

In appointing J.C. to the position of captain there were several laudatory contributions from officials and members. Two of these expressed the view that Jack White was a very unselfish individual, and they were concerned that, as captain, he would not bowl himself enough. Indeed, one requested of other team members that they should ensure that White should not be allowed to underbowl himself. There must have been some under the breath mutterings at that, because one or two of his colleagues thought that he had too much of the bowling. In later years, when tackled on the subject, he responded, *"Well cock, they can't seem to hit me, so it seems sensible to continue."*

Captaincy seems to have been the trigger which transformed Jack White into a useful batsman. Perhaps it was the onus or desire to show others what was needed, perhaps he thought that he owed it to his position of captain. From the first game, a trial match for the County possibles, he displayed batting skills which previously had appeared only occasionally. The Rest in the trial were all out for 145, and the prospective County eleven were wobbling at 80 for 6 when he joined A.E. Rippon at the wicket. He proceeded to score 38 and saw the first-innings lead established.

The season was not an unbridled success for Somerset; they won four matches and lost nine, with thirteen drawn. In the review of the season in the Somerset Gazette in September, the non-availability of the amateurs was commented upon. Hunt and Young were still the regular professionals and they had been joined notably by Jack Lee and Luckes, a wicket-keeper, but dependency on the amateurs remained. White was said to be a popular skipper, and the Gazette, almost as an afterthought, as though it was saying the obvious and it was unnecessary, wrote that *"White, of course, is still the finest amateur slow bowler in the Country."*

1927 was also the year when a future Somerset legend made his first appearance. Arthur Wellard was brought down from Kent to embark on two years residential qualification, but of course he was unable to play in the championship matches.

Wisden was extremely complimentary to White and wrote, *"Having regard to the limitations of the side in every particular, it is scarcely an exaggeration to say that J.C. White carried Somerset upon his shoulders. The undertaking of new duties as captain of the side in no way prejudiced his all-round ability or his capacity for hard work. In addition to increasing his batting aggregate by about 300 runs and averaging 23, he was nearly as effective as ever with the ball."*

The season, after a good start, turned out to be one of the worst ever for rain, and many fixtures were ruined by it. A memorable game was that against Gloucestershire at Taunton. Somerset were 140 for 4 when White and C.C.C. Case came together, and they had the satisfaction of both scoring their maiden first-class centuries. They were both undefeated at the end of one day, having put on 240 runs together in three hours. A large crowd turned up the next day, a Bank Holiday, hoping to see the slaughter continue, but within eleven minutes both were back in the pavilion, White having scored a chanceless 113 and Case 122. Rain stopped play on the final day and the game ended in a draw.

Walter Hammond didn't have a bad game either. He scored 197 (bowled White) out of 331 in the first innings and had made an umdefeated 58 out of 125 for 3 in the second innings when rain brought a premature halt to the proceedings. The Somerset Gazette showed its impartiality by giving Hammond the headlines. As he scored many centuries, it seems a little unfair that the two Somerset men could not have had their glory on that particular day. C.C.C. Case, with the wonderful nickname of "Box", scored a lot of useful runs for Somerset, but will always be remembered for the occasion he faced Larwood at Trent Bridge, when the latter was racing in with a good head of steam. Trying to evade a lifter, Case dropped his bat and then stood on his wickets. In his confusion, he then departed at pace for the pavilion carrying a stump instead of his bat. The story reminds me of the Somerset tail-ender facing a bowler of considerable speed, who was making the ball fly to a disconcerting degree. After a couple of zoomers, he groped at a ball which was outside the off-stump, and then set off for the pavilion. *"Just a minute"*, said the umpire, *"You didn't touch it"*. *"Near enough for me, thank you"*, came the reply, *"Good day"*.

Somerset didn't win a match until the Worcester fixture in mid-June. Somerset won by an innings and later that month repeated the medicine but, this time winning by an innings and 199 runs, White taking eight wickets including the last three of the game in four balls.

At Bath, White demonstrated his batting abilities when scoring 56 not out in two and a half hours without a chance, to halt a batting collapse against Yorkshire. Among his notable bowling performances that summer was 8 for 28 in 22 overs against the New Zealanders at Weston-super-Mare. At Lords against Middlesex, he played like a real all-rounder and scored 70 and 65 and took 6 for 89.

White again topped the County bowling averages, this time with 112 wickets for 2063 runs off 1182 overs at an average of 18.41. What must have given him as much pleasure was his batting. He had scored the first century of his first-class career, and scored 841 runs at an average of 22.13.

After the previous year's financial success, it was sad to report that Somerset had a deficit of £1500, a considerable amount of money in those days. It was also sad that the stalwart John Daniell announced his retirement. Not many players can have given more to the County than the popular ex-captain. Apart from his playing career in both rugby and cricket, he held important administrative posts, being a President of the Rugby Football Union and successively secretary and President of Somerset C.C.C.

Elsewhere in the country, the first wireless cricket commentary broadcast took place in Essex. Marvellous, it had taken us five more years to do something which Australia did in 1922!

Very far apart, two young men were starting their careers with a bang. In England, Walter Hammond equalled the W.G. Grace achievement of scoring 1000 runs in May, in 22 days to be precise. Whilst in Adelaide, a young New South Wales colt called Bradman scored a century in his very first Sheffield Shield match.

The West Indians had toured England on previous occasions, but in 1928 they were granted Test match status and, as Maurice Tate unwittingly wrote in his autobiography, *"we awarded them the honour of three Test Matches."* He committed another faux pas in his book when he reported how Tich Freeman routed the West Indians, *"to the confusion of the darkies."* And Maurice was considered to be a man of the people! It was still very much a white man's world at that time. He writes that he couldn't remember much about the final Test with the West Indies because his thoughts were already very much on the forthcoming visit to Australia. To quote him: *"This is just another proof that the only real Test matches are those between England and Australia. In their own countries, in their peculiar climactic conditions, and with M.C.C. teams not truly representative, we have lost Tests in South Africa and the West Indies. But at home we have never lost a Test against any country other than Australia. That should tell its own story."* Oh dear, how poor Maurice would turn in his grave if he knew of the happenings of the last decade or two.

In fact, England did win all three matches against the Indies that year, quite comfortably, and in spite of the efforts of the majestic Learie Constantine, the first of a long line of West Indies batsmen who would entertain the crowds for generations thereafter. The black man might still struggle for equality in some spheres, but in cricket - oh no - that was more than achieved some years ago.

I have been unable to discover exactly why it happened, but J.C. White was suddenly back in the eyes of the selectors, and he played in the second of the West Indies Tests with the creditable performance of 3 wickets for 53 runs off 27.3 overs at an average of 17.66. England won the game by an innings, scoring 351, against West Indies 206 and 115. Jack White scored 21 not out, and took over the captaincy when Percy Chapman had to retire hurt. Maybe his selection was because the selectors knew that he was available to tour Australia in the coming winter. Sir Home Gordon claimed some responsibility, stating that Jack White had voiced regrets of not being able to accept invitations to tour in the past and that he doubted that now he was available that he would be selected. Sir Home asked permission to pass the knowledge on to the relevant people. Famous cricketers, past and present, had been unanimous in advocating White's inclusion for the coming Australian tour, claiming that he could bowl all day on shirt-front wickets, keeping the runs down at one end whilst the fast bowlers were taking it in turns to get wickets at the other end.

It may have been the fact that he had been turning out winning performances for longer than most other bowlers. He was the only bowler playing in 1928 who had taken more than 100 wickets every year since the First World War.

He had been invited to play in the Gentlemen v Players match at Lords. All the critics praised his steadiness in that match, bowling a good length on a perfect wicket, and they also complimented him upon his fielding. Colonel Trevor in the Telegraph wrote that White kept an immaculate length but he could not persuade the leading professional batsmen of the country (who know him well) to take liberties. H.C. Littlewort of the Daily Chronicle stated that White was easily the most competent attacker on the Gentlemen side.

Incidentally, there were two Somerset amateurs invited to play for the Gentlemen that year. The other one was none other than M.D. Lyon! So there must have been some healing of the wounds between him and the M.C.C. The notice in the press announcing the match stated that the following had been invited to play and then gave a list of the names. Two items of interest there. The first was that eleven names only were selected for each side, no reserves or stand-bys. The second was the statement that captains would be chosen when replies have been received! As the notice in the papers was posted only a few days before the actual match, it suggests a somewhat more casual approach than would be the case for such an important fixture today.

There is another possible reason for White's inclusion in the Test side that year. Although Somerset lost to Middlesex, White had the very good match figures of 6 for 77 off 47 overs and 6 for 73 off 29.3 overs. Don't forget that he had a very good game there the previous year also. No fool, our Jack. As Patsy Hendren said, there is nothing so certain to get a batsman into a Test side as scoring hundreds. The selectors cannot ignore a good run of those. In the same vein, a bowler with oodles of wickets has to be seriously considered. Jack White had oodles of wickets, but where better to emphasise the fact than at Lords, the headquarters of cricket, and probably in front of the people who mattered most when it came to selecting teams for the future.

In Somerset, the 1928 A.G.M. had revealed the sad news that the previous year had resulted in a four-figure financial loss. When one considers that the 1926 total income for the year was only £3000, this must have come as a considerable shock to the chairman and shareholders. Poor Mr. Davey, the secretary, who had been praised for his good housekeeping only twelve months previously, his star must have waned hugely. The financial shock called for drastic action, and that is exactly what it got. The management tore the previous year's fixture list apart, and incredibly decided to delete the fixtures with Yorkshire and Lancashire, and surprisingly include a fixture with Nottinghamshire. The logic escapes me, but there must have been such. Travelling would have been reduced to an extent, but one would have thought that matches against the red and white rose counties would have produced large gates of paying customers.

Even more unpopular was the decision to not play any home matches at Bath, Knowle, and Weston-super-mare until August. Apparently the gates at those venues had not justified the extra expense of moving away from the main County ground at Taunton. In the first three months of the season, there were only five home matches, and these were all played at Taunton. The traditional Whitsuntide Bank Holiday fixture was changed to an alternative date on the pretext that Somerset and Gloucestershire people will attend to witness the local derby on any date, and therefore the Bank Holiday could be used to encourage the paying public to a less popular fixture.

The Somerset Gazette reported that Jack White, in his first season as skipper, had many anxious hours, and it was unlikely that they would be any less in the coming season as equal talent to the retiring or departing John Daniell, P.R. Johnson, M.D. Lyon, and J.C.W. MacBryan would be hard to find. Analysis of Somerset's batting over the previous years reveals just how much it had depended on those four gentlemen.

J.C. had one experience in June of that year which he would have rather done without. It wasn't that unusual for someone, now and again, to hit him for six, but nine times out of ten they paid for their temerity very quickly afterwards. We have already seen that the left-handed Woolley played him better than most, and perhaps it was watching Woolley which persuaded Les Ames to have a go - with some result. He hit Jack for three sixes in four balls! The following week J.C. experienced something far more unique. Somerset were playing Hampshire, and White was bowling to Creese, a South African who had qualified for Hampshire only the day before. White beat him in the flight and removed the off-bail, which proceeded to hit the wicket-keeper Luckes' gloves and bounced back to reset itself perfectly on the stumps. The batsman was unaware of what had happened and both umpires claimed to have been unsighted and therefore gave "not out". Creese's relief was terribly short-lived, for White bowled him the very next ball.

Wisden, reporting on the 1928 season, once more praised White on his captaincy of the Somerset team. *"In his second season as leader of the eleven, J.C. White earned great distinction, both as captain and as the mainstay of the side. Upon his shoulders fell the chief weight of the bowling, and although the fielding at times proved of indifferent quality, he performed so consistently that for the tenth successive year he secured more than one hundred wickets. His sound batting too, helped in more than one recovery from a wretched start. . . ."* Again J.C.'s abilities are demonstrated by the bowling analyses he produced in matches in which Somerset were soundly beaten. Examples are the games against Sussex, Warwickshire, Middlesex, and Glamorgan. Somerset were handsomely defeated on each occasion, but Jack White took 12, 10, 12, and 12 wickets respectively.

In 1928, the forthcoming great airliners of the world were pure "sci-fi" and travel across the oceans was still by ship, a more prolonged experience, taking of the order of six weeks from England to Perth. It was therefore necessary to select the winter touring party to Australia in August before the English season had even finished. Those who went initially had to be relied upon. There was no opportunity in those days for a replacement to be flown out if someone broke down with a bad back or other ailment.

There was much rejoicing in Somerset when the M.C.C. party for Australia was announced and it was learned that J.C. "Farmer" White had been included as vice-captain to the popular Percy Chapman. The Somerst Gazette reported, *"West Country cricket enthusiasts in general and Somerset people in particular will applaud the wisdom and foresight of the M.C.C. Selection Committee who met at Lord's on Monday night to select the players to participate in the forthcoming tour to Australia and who decided to include John Cornish White among the favoured few, bringing him in as vice-captain. For the past three months the sporting Press of the country has been going all out in favour of the Somerset captain's inclusion in the team to defend the famous 'Ashes', and though the selection committee has in years past been somewhat apathetic concerning the claims of West country cricketers, Mr. White has now the opportunity of proving his worth, as no doubt he will do. . . ."* The article continued with some references to J.C.'s achievements and his abilities, and also waxed lyrical about bygone days when Jack was 'nowt but a lad': *"One remembers Jack White as a boy, coming to Dunster with Captain Byrne, the late Jack Hellard and the two Greswells, who all used to play for Stogumber - in the leisurely pre-war days. He was a wonderful bowler then and some of his balls used to come off the ground like flushed snipe. Since those days when the local curate gave a home batsman in when he was very likely out, Jack White has gone far."*

There was an element of truth in the assertion that chaps from the West country had to be better than good before they were selected for their Country. Charlie Parker would say "Amen" to that; but the chaps from the northern counties would argue likewise. Those players based in the home counties seemed to have an advantage; but when the team selected for Australia that year is considered, too much prejudice is not apparent. There were three Kent players, two each from Surrey, Lancashire, and Yorkshire, and one each from Gloucestershire, Middlesex, Hampshire, Nottinghamshire, Sussex, Somerset, and Leicestershire. A pretty good spread of representation from the various first-class counties.

I doubt whether the selectors have yet been born who would pick a side to satisfy every critic, but they were not too far adrift on this occasion. The main criticism was that Frank Woolley had not been included and Pelham Warner, in later years, admitted that this was probably a mistake, although in the event Woolley was not missed. Apart from his undoubted skills, Woolley would have provided the all-rounder which some argued the team lacked. Dependency on Hammond as a back-up bowler did not rest easily with some critics. It is strange that Woolley was not chosen as of course he was Percy Chapman's Kent colleague. Some suggested that Chapman was jealous of Woolley, but others stoutly dismissed this idea as absolute nonsense. Perhaps there was something in their characters which did not quite gel, certainly Woolley was a quiet man whilst Chapman was full of bonhomie. The more likely reason for his exclusion is that the selectors, not Chapman, did not pick him, and Chapman was out-manoeuvred. So Woolley was left at home, the same Woolley of whom Robertson-Glasgow wrote, *"there was all summer in a stroke by Woolley, and he batted as it is sometimes shown in dreams"*.

7.

AUSTRALIAN EXPERIENCE

ON A THURSDAY in late September, some two thousand people gathered at Victoria station to bid the English warriors well as they set forth on the first stage of their crusade. The knights were minus their armour of course and not all easily distinguishable in the milling throng, but Percy Chapman's mother soon put that right by pinning to the lapel of each player a sprig of white heather tied with a ribbon. Chapman was presented with a huge horseshoe in M.C.C. colours, decorated with white heather, and he obligingly hung it around his neck as he leaned out of the window to wave his farewell from the departing express.

A small advance party had left a day or two before, but all were bound for Toulon where they were to board the Orient liner "Otranto". Seventeen players were in the party, and F.C. Toone was the manager. There were also a few companions, including Percy Chapman's wife, Beet. The press corps was also in attendance.

The tour had not been arranged without some difficulties. The Australian Board of Control at the time was not the most proficient, and was not a match for autocratic M.C.C. There had been disquiet at Lord's, when the Australian Board had refused to accommodate England's request for two matches in New Zealand to be scheduled into the tour. The M.C.C. secretary, William Findlay, then wrote regretting that the Board had seen fit to arrange to play one of the Tests at Brisbane, rather than two in Sydney. The Board had been promising Queensland a Test ever since its formation in 1905 and now Lord's was objecting. A new pitch had been laid there by the Melbourne Cricket ground curator, and it was an insult for M.C.C. to suggest that the venue was other than acceptable. Eventually M.C.C. imperiously acceded to the proposal with the following reply, *"It is assumed that your Board when making its decision has thoroughly considered the matter and in the circumstances the Marylebone Cricket Club committee do not feel justified in making any objection."* Did they go out of their way to annoy and antagonise people. I think not; they simply considered themselves THE administrators of cricket and all things connected therewith!

The demands which M.C.C. put upon the Australian Board regarding the tour took up many hours in the Board's meetings, and is said to have cost the Board and hence the state associations a considerable amount of money.

The M.C.C. manager for the tour, Frederick Toone, the Yorkshire secretary, was making his third trip to Australia, and was a master of detail. His managerial skills left his Australian counterparts floundering. Toone was knighted soon after the tour was completed but unfortunately had but a short time to enjoy this honour as he died in 1930.

The England team was considered a strong one and their hopes of retaining the "Ashes" was high. The Australians were going through a transitional period, and the fast bowling department was not strong. The English team comprised Percy Chapman of Kent as captain, and J.C. White of Somerset as vice-captain. The batsmen were Jack Hobbs (Surrey), Herbert Sutcliffe (Yorks), Patsy Hendren (Middx), D.R. Jardine (Surrey), Maurice Leyland (Yorks), C.P. Mead (Hants), and Ernest Tyldesley (Lancs). The wicket-keepers were George Duckworth (Lancs) and Les Ames (Kent). The bowlers (other than White) were Harold Larwood (Notts), George Geary (Leics), Percy Freeman (Kent), and Sam Staples (Notts). The all-rounders were Maurice Tate (Sussex) and Wally Hammond (Gloucs).

Percy Chapman, as captain, could not have been bettered. He was an outgoing personality who had the ability to mix on all levels. He was not short of a little repartee when needed and was the stuff that ambassadors are made of, or should be. Importantly, he was respected by the team members, indeed almost adored by some of them. He had a rapport with the Australian press and people, and even when he did something which they did not like, he had the ability to ensure that it was soon forgotten and not allowed to fester. There is little doubt that he was at the pinnacle of his career. Arthur Percy Frank Chapman had been born to lead England. His father was no mean cricketer himself, and played for Rutland, Lincolnshire, Radnor, Shropshire and Berkshire. Indeed, he once claimed to have played for them all in successive weeks! When Percy was at Oakham school he scored a century and wrote to his father asking him if he would like to reward him by sending a bat. His father jokingly sent him the bat with which he had played on the garden lawn when he was four years old. It had only half a blade, to suit his height at that age. Percy wrote back, *"I want to get another century, not 50."*

At Uppingham school his cricketing deeds were legendary. One afternoon House matches were being played and it is alleged that he was eligible for both his junior team and the senior team. He played for the seniors and scored a hundred which helped them to win the Cup. He then cycled down to where the juniors were playing and discovered that they were being beaten with only the tail-enders left to bat. He went in at the fall of the next wicket, farmed the bowling, scored a second century of the afternoon, and won the Cup for the Juniors. Boy's Own stuff, if ever there was.

The young Chapman was good at any sport he turned his hand to. By coincidence, he was a great friend of M.D. Lyon, who you will remember from his contretemps with the M.C.C., and together they beat the Cambridge University top tennis pair. They followed this by challenging two golf Blues and put them to the sword, in spite of the fact that Chapman arrived for the game with only three clubs in his bag. The so-called Golden Age of Cricket, before the First World War, was probably the era which would have suited Chapman best, when the game was played at pace but with a nonchalant air of well-being. Certainly the thirties and thereafter, when hundreds had to be earned and were ground out after long stays at the wicket, would not have been his forte. He enjoyed his cricket and his batting reflected that, bright and breezy would not be inappropriate.

He had celebrated his 28th birthday not long before the touring side had set forth from England, so in cricketing terms he was extremely young to be honoured with the captaincy in an age when it was usual for many of the players to continue into their forties and even fifties. Some would say that he was past his best. As a young man he had been tall, willowy and lithe, but as an amateur he had to have an income and his chosen career was the whisky trade. In later life his drinking was to be his downfall, leading to the break-up of what had been a very happy marriage, and his condition would embarrass his friends increasingly until many resorted to avoiding him and increasingly he remained at his lodgings, which were the home of Bernard Benson, the steward at West Hill golf club. Even towards the end of his life he could not forego the amber tipple, and when Les Ames and Hopper Levett, two erstwhile team-mates, visited him they were pleased to find that he had only a half-pint glass in his hand. On leaving they indicated to Bernard Benson that weaning Percy off the hard stuff on to halves of beer was an improvement surely, only to be informed that they had not realised that it was whisky in the glass.

But those were times still in the future; in 1928 Percy was still a captain to be respected by his own men and the opposition alike. His batting was free and aggressive, if sometimes brittle, and he was still admired as one of the best catchers in the business. In earlier days he had been a fielder par excellence, wherever he was stationed, but by 1928 he had begun to put on weight and he restricted himself to positions nearer to the bat. For Jack White in international cricket, Chapman played exactly the role which John Daniell had played in County cricket. He fielded at silly point or in the gully and with his tremendous reach and large hands he snapped up many chances which others would have considered impossible.

Chapman demonstrated his ambassadorial skills the moment the team disembarked at Fremantle. A dock worker called out to him, *"Good luck Chapman. Have you brought the Ashes with you?"* Back went the reply, quick as a flash, *"Yes, I have. I will show them to you on the way back."* *"I'll have a quid with you on that,"* shouted the docker. *"I'll take it,"* replied Chapman, *"and collect it on the way home."* It was exactly what the Australians liked. They loved to indulge in a little verbal barracking, but were just as pleased when the victim responded in like manner. Maurice Tate was one of those who almost worshipped Chapman, and he testified to Chapman's appeal. *"Whatever he did, whoever he caught miraculously, he was received as a sport - fair dinkum, they call it Down Under. We who played under Percy Chapman loved him, and the pure dyed-in-the-wool backwoods Australians, who trekked hundreds of miles to see Australia beat England even in one Test match, respected him."*

The team which had been assembled to assist Chapman in his task was formidable, each player was of proven ability, many at Test match level, and all had already starred on numerous occasions on the County grounds of England. It seems inconceivable that in 1998/99 a party set forth, with the same aims in mind, and the Old Country could not produce one spin bowler of real merit, most of the fast men were unproven, and the batsmen were selected more because they were better than others than because their performances demanded it.

It is not intended to give cameos of all the players, though each would make enthralling reading, but some mention should be made of a man whose batting was to rival, or should we say, complement Jack White's bowling. Walter Hammond was one of the younger members of the team, in 1928 he was still only 25 years of age, but his feats in the previous three years were such that cricket lovers felt that he had been on the cricketing stage much longer.

The greatest tribute to Hammond's talents come from none other than Sir Leonard Hutton, and you can't go much higher than that in the cricket world. Hutton wrote that Hammond *"was the finest batsman that I played with or against."* Well, Hutton never played with or against Grace, but he did play against Bradman! Furthermore, Hutton wrote those words in 1983, so they weren't an off the cuff observation.

Hammond was another who had taken to cricket at an early stage. His father was an army man and Walter's early life was spent at various postings culminating at Malta, where they were to be found at the outbreak of the 1914-18 war. They returned to England, and when his father was posted to France, his mother decided that Walter might benefit from a boarding education and so he was sent to Cirencester Grammar school as a boarder. His father, who had encouraged him in his cricket, was killed in the last days of the war whilst Walter was still at school. He dominated the cricket scene at the school, and in one House match scored 365 not out, including 24 sixes and 34 fours. His batting average in the House matches that year was 613. He had played four innings and been out only once. His bowling was also outstanding, and he took 25 wickets at an average of 2.00. Yes, 2.00! But that was all shoolboy cricket and could it be transformed to success at a higher level. Although several watchers claimed to see that potential at an early stage of his career, his first years with Gloucestershire were none too promising, at least as far as results are concerned. In 1921, he played three innings for the County, admittedly all against the Australians, and scored two runs for a first-class average of 0.66.

Early in 1922, Lord Harris, who had affiliations with Kent where Hammond was born, challenged his qualification to play for Gloucestershire. Schooldays did not count for residency qualification, and Hammond found himself having to wait until 1923, when his residency period expired, before he could play again for his adopted county. In 1923 he scored a century in the opening game against Surrey, and followed that with 92 in the second innings. He scored 1300 runs that summer, but still had scored only one first-class hundred. Now Patsy Hendren said that it is scoring hundreds and nothing else which gets batsmen selected for representative matches, and I am sure that is usually the case, but Hammond was something out of the ordinary and, more importantly, influential people were observing such. Cardus became a devotee and also Pelham Warner, and both enhanced Hammond's career prospects with glowing reports of his talents. Indeed, with only one first-class hundred to his credit, he was selected to play for the Players against the Gentlemen. 1924 and 1925 were good but unexceptional seasons for Hammond, until mid-August of the latter year when he blossomed mightily at Old Trafford against a Lancashire attack which included the Australian fast bowler Ted McDonald. He scored 250, and fortunately for Hammond and all posterity, Cardus was there to witness the deed. He wrote:

"Yesterday was the gladdest day I have spent on a cricket field for many years. The cricketers of Grace's county came to dour Old Trafford and brought with them tidings of joy and comfort. Young Walter Hammond of Gloucestershire played one of the finest innings that can ever have been accomplished by a boy of his age.

"To be present at the rising of a star in the sky and to know it is going to be glorious - here is a moment thrilling indeed to men who live their lives imaginatively. It was as plain as the nose on Bardolph's face that Hammond is an England batsman of tomorrow. In years to come we will remember August 19th 1925 at Old Trafford for when in good time Hammond carves history out of Australian bowlers here and across the seas, we shall be proud to say that we understood well enough he was born for the company of master batsmen." Well, master Hammond could hardly fail after that, nor did he.

In the winter of 1925/26 he was chosen to tour the West Indies, and a mosquito bite or some other ailment almost ended his life. On returning to England, he spent many months in Bristol Royal Infirmary, threatened at one stage with the amputation of his leg. Thus 1926 passed by with Hammond hors de combat. The following year he made amends, equalling Grace's record of 1000 runs in May. After that runs simply flowed (nay, poured) from his bat.

Thus, he arrived in Australia, full of runs and a trump card in England's hand. But, as we have seen with Percy Chapman, off the field performance can be as important as on the field. How did Hammond stand up in that direction? He was a fairly reserved character, almost shy with those he did not know. Sometimes this was misinterpreted, particularly by those of an extrovert nature who were unable to appreciate that others may not be of similar character to themselves. In the Gloucestershire dressing rooms, remembering that the amateurs and professionals were segregated, he did not appear to sit easily in either camp. He was a professional, no doubt, but in some ways seemed more suited to being an amateur. Thus he made few close friends within cricket, and sometimes was unfairly criticised as being stand-offish, whereas in reality he was simply reserved. He was also a very modest man. However, he was sociable enough, had a quiet humour, and was not averse to a little horseplay on occasions. In other words, an average tourist. But his batting, there was nothing "average" about that, as the Australians were soon to learn.

It is not always essential that a team shall be a happy party off the field of play if they are to prosper on it. The Bodyline Series in 1932/33 is an example of that. The team on that occasion was divided on the morality of using bodyline bowling tactics and this resulted in disquiet off the field. Jardine, as captain, had but one thought in mind, to win the Ashes, and he had decided how that could be achieved. If that led to a less than harmonious party on the tour, too bad. He was not in Australia on a diplomatic mission, far from it. But England did win.

Percy Chapman, on the other hand, was automatically on a diplomatic mission, that was his character. Cricket was important, and he would do his darnedest to ensure that England retained the coveted trophy, but if they did not - too bad; it was more important that everyone had enjoyed themselves, including the Australians. However, he did have a happy party, and that was in no small way due to his generous and warm personality.

Hobbs and Sutcliffe went together like stawberries and cream, a hugely experienced and successful opening partnership. They were elder statesmen of the party, giving a degree of quiet seriousness to proceedings, a calming influence if matters were getting out of hand. Hobbs with his innocuous superstitions, and Sutcliffe, serene and debonair. As Robertson-Glasgow once wrote, *"The sort of man who would rather miss a train than run for it and be seen in disorder and heard breathing heavily."*

Incidentally, Hendren in his little autobiographical book, "Big Cricket", wrote of batsmen helping each other when batting. One man might not be too keen on facing a leg-spinner at the beginning of his innings, for example; and his partner would take that end until the other man had his eye in. The surprising thing is that Patsy suggests that this happens at the very top of the tree, and he instances Hobbs shielding Sutcliffe from the bowling at the Oval in 1926, when the pair of them eventually laid the foundations for an England victory which won the Ashes. Patsy stated that he knows the Yorkshireman would agree that Jack Hobbs helped him on that and other occasions.

Any touring party needs a comedian or two to lighten up the proceedings and provide a little entertainment. Patsy Hendren, an impish man with a kind heart, not averse to a little slapstick, would oblige in that direction; ably, or should it be loudly, supported by George Duckworth, a noisy character, full of gusto and rough humour. Maurice Tate would weigh in also, he was a talker, an enthusiast, who could soon be persuaded to play his part in any little bit of nonsense.

On the quieter side were men like Larwood, who was only twenty-three and was very much minding his "p's and q's", on his first visit to the Antipodes. C.P. Mead the dour Hampshire left-hander, would doubtless be one of those in the background, unless a crisis was brewing, when he would be seen moving unhurriedly but purposefully to the fore. Mead was a professional's man, an accumulator of runs, not a crowd-pleaser, though he had his moments. He was unhurried at the crease, and went through a routine of toe-wiggling, cap tweaking, etc. before facing each ball. He was solid and indestructible when batting, and no doubt very dependable off the field.

Les Ames would be an asset to any touring side, a courteous and friendly man, a team man who respected the gifts of others not envied them. He had a few gifts himself; in 1928 he had scored 1919 runs and taken 121 dismissals behind the stumps!

Douglas Jardine is always painted as autocratic and aloof and combative, but he was a very thorough and observant person and had a dry wit, and must have played his part at the more upper-class social events where some of the professionals might have felt a little ill at ease.

What contribution did Jack White make? He was not a noted conversationalist, but he did understand etiquette and was polite and affable. As a countryman, he was also able to talk intelligently about the farming and country scene in Britain, subjects which would find ready listeners in Australia. He was said to be popular with his team-mates and also the Australian public. There are recorded instances of his indulgence in light-hearted pranks as testament to the fact that he did let his hair down on occasion. Basically a quiet man, he appears to have fitted well into the off-field team and performed his vice-captaincy duties creditably.

Yes, England had a team to be reckoned with, but the tourists were faced with difficulties right from the start as poor Sam Staples developed muscular back-trouble on the boat, could not shake off the ailment, and was soon allowed to return home without having had the pleasure of turning his arm over. In the first match, George Geary was hit in the face and was out of action for a month. Thus, the playing squad had been reduced to fifteen. Chapman had demonstrated his skills in diplomacy in that very first match, when he went out to bat wearing the cap of the Western Australia Incogniti, of which he had just been elected a life member. It was the sort of public relations exercise which the crowd appreciated.

In the second match of the tour against South Australia, Chapman hit 145 runs in only two and a quarter hours, taking eighteen off one Grimmett over. It was exactly what was needed at that juncture of the tour, as it demonstrated that he was as worth his position as captain of the team on the field, as undoubtedly he was, with his charm and good humour, off the field. It allowed him to relax from concerns about his batting and concentrate on his ambassadorial role, and the whole team and the tour benefited from it.

In the match against New South Wales, England were to meet for the first time a man who would prove to be a thorn in the side for many years to come - Bradman. The Don announced himself with 87 and 132 not out in that match. The match was drawn and England's batsmen also showed their mettle, declaring at 734 for 7, with big scores from Hammond 225, Hendren 167, and Jardine 140.

The first Test duly arrived and it is important to remember that these were to be timeless Tests. It was played at Brisbane, commencing on the 30th November, the first time that a Test match had been played in that city, and much to the delight of Queenslanders, no doubt. It was also agreed that there should be six-ball overs, presumably at the persuasion of M.C.C.. Chapman and his selectors, White, Jardine, Hobbs and Tyldesley, opted for a strong batting line-up, and there was some consternation in the English press when it was seen that Geary and Freeman had been left out.

The discussion over White's inclusion and Freeman's exclusion must have been interesting, to say the least. They both spun the ball away from the right-handers, Freeman with his leg-breaks and White with his left-arm off-breaks. Against Freeman was the fact that White was one of the selectors, and all other things being equal, it would be unlikely that the other selectors would argue too strongly for Freeman to the disadvantage of White. Also White was an amateur, one of only three in the touring party, and this was a time when the amateurs still enjoyed some priority treatment over their professional colleagues. It was still inconceivable that a professional should lead the side for example. Moreover, White was the designated vice-captain. There was also a feeling that good as Freeman was in England, he did not spread the same alarm and despondency amongst Australian batsmen. There were two reasons for this view. The first was that every Australian club-side had its leg-breaker, and therefore they were used to the wiles of such exponents. Secondly, Freeman had been to Australia with the previous tour, under Arthur Gilligan, and had not "pulled up any trees".

It has to be remembered also that Chapman and Freeman were both members of the Kent side. Freeman must have been championed for inclusion in the touring party by Chapman, so he must have had a few misgivings in not insisting that he should be included in the Test team. The selection committee sat late into the evening in choosing the team, but what the items were which kept them talking do not appear to have been made public.

The preference of Jack White against Percy Freeman tells us something of the quality and standing of White. Freeman was a marvellous performer and repeatedly produced amazing analyses. For example, in his career he took more than thirteen wickets in a match on no less than forty occasions, and over his career he averaged 209 wickets per season. It was said, however, that the very best batsmen overcame him by the quick use of their feet. Well, there are a few Kentish men (or should it be men of Kent) who might puff their cheeks out at that suggestion.

On the Australian side Bradman, at twenty years of age, was making his Test debut, but he was the only youngster to be selected. At the other end of the scale, at forty-six but claiming to be forty-one, was Ironmonger, also making his debut. There were facets of this game which would make present-day Englishmen and Australians alike blink with incredulity. Firstly, it was acknowledged that the Englishmen were much the better fielding side. Secondly, although the British press criticised England for having a long tail, it actually performed more like a 1999 Australian tail, i.e. it contributed runs. Larwood, for example, only just missed his century on two occasions and had a batting average over the course of the tour of over 26. The whole side had batting averages in double figures. For once the butts of the jokes were the Australians. Ironside always batted immediately above the extras and never scored anywhere near as many runs as them. The

"Every season from 1919 to 1932. John Cornish White took over a hundred wickets and twice scored more than a thousand runs.

His slow left handed bowling, with flight, variation of pace and break, maintained with tireless accuracy, has lured many great batsmen to disaster.

In 1921, when he took all ten Worcestershire wickets, he played for England at Leeds.

Touring Australia (1928/9) he dismissed 25 men in the five tests. He captained England in the last match and also three more times against South Africa in 1929.

Batting right handed he can defend or force a game."

"No other County captain has to bear a larger share of the bowling than the Somerset leader.

Slow left hand, with a high delivery, White became a regular member of the county eleven in 1913, and in every season since the War he has taken a hundred or more wickets.

Remarkably accurate length and an abundance of spin make him deadly on turf affected by rain.

Played for England against Australia and several times for the Gentlemen; also went with an MCC team to South America, 1926-27.

Smart slip fielding and his ability to bat well increase his value to Somerset."

J.C. White immortalised on cigarette cards.

Somerset 1901, famously beat Yorkshire by scoring 630 in their second innings.
Gill, Robson, Braund, G Barrington, FA Phillips, AE Newton, SMJ Woods,
LCH Palairet, MT Hill, Cranfield, Lewis.

John Daniell, Somerset captain batting in a trademark homburg..

E.J. Tyler.

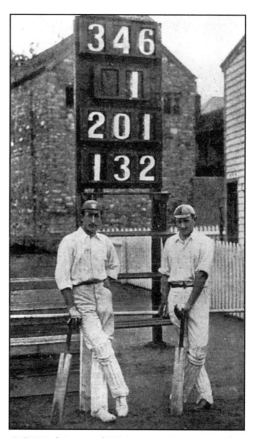

LCH Palairet and HT Hewett in 1892, after their world record opening partnership of 346.

J.Daniell.

E.Robson.

A.E.S.Rippon.

WORCESTERSHIRE

First Innings

1	Bowley	c Lowry b White	1
2	Pearson (F)	c and b White	74
3	Turner (R.E.)	b White	12
4	Mr.H.L.Higgins	lbw b White	16
5	Mr.M.F.S.Sewell	st Chidgey b White	66
6	Mr.W.E.Richardson	b White	7
7	Preece (C.A.)	c Daniell b White	27
8	Tarbox (C.V.)	b White	13
9	Mr.C.H.B.Parsonby	lbw b White	0
10	Mr.V.W.Humpherson	not out	2
11	Mr.H.A.Gilbert	c Hope b White	0
		b 14 l-b 5 w n-b	19

Total 237

Fall of the wickets

1-4   2-47   3-81   4-106   5-127   6-182   7-222
8-222   9-237   10-237

Bowling analysis

	O	M	R	W	W-4	N-b
Robson	25	4	71	0		
Mr.White	42.2	11	76	10		
Hunt	18	4	55			
Mr.Wharton	6	2	16			

Somerset V Worcestershire —— June 18-21 1921.
JC White took all 10 wickets as Somerset won by 83 runs.

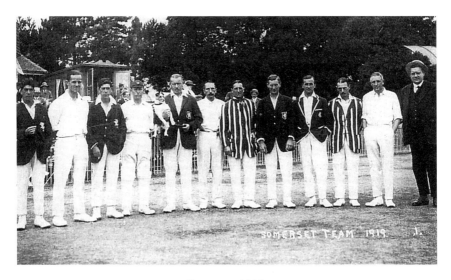

Somerset 1919.
S Rippon, J Bridges, D Rippon, Chidgey, Poyntz(holding dog), Robson, Daniell, White, N Hardy, MacBryan, Braund, Scott, McAuley(scorer).

MCC on tour in South America 1926/27. White is 5th from the left.

Australia: Kippax, Oxenham, Ponsford, Hele(umpire), Kelleway, Gregory, Hendry, Ironmonger, Elder(umpire), Oldfield, Grimmett, Ryder(capt), Bradman, Woodfull.
1928/29 Ashes Teams.
England: Duckworth, Ames, Mead, Tate, Hendren, Leyland, Staples, Hammond, Toone (manager), Sutcliffe, Larwood, Freeman, Tyldesley, White, Chapman(capt), Jardine, Hobbs.

The Old Firm.
Sutcliffe and Hobbs going in to open England's innings in the second test match
at Sydney in December 1928.

BOWLER	WKTS	RUNS
BRADMAN		
KIPPAX		11
RICHARDSON		
WOODFULL		
RYDER		22
BLACKIE	4	148
IRONMONGER	2	142
GRIMMETT	2	191
HENDRY	1	52
NOTHLING		60

AUS. IST INGS	253
ENG. IST INGS	636

BATSMEN	
DUCKWORTH	39
WHITE	29
10 FOR	636

BATSMEN	OUT	F OF W
SUTCLIFFE	11	37
HOBBS	40	65
JARDINE	28	148
HENDREN	74	293
CHAPMAN	20	341
LARWOOD	43	432
HAMMOND	251	496
TATE	25	523
GEARY	66	592
SUNDRIES	10	

The Record Test Score. The Adelaide scoreboard after England's first innings in the fourth test, February 1929.

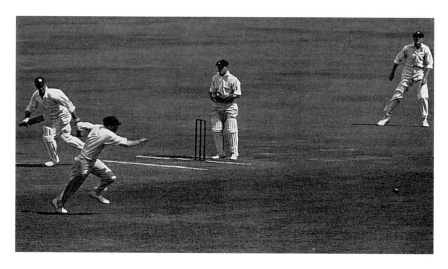

White makes the winning run with a tap to the on off Nothling.

ENGLAND

J.B.Hobbs	c Ryder b Hendry	74	c Oldfield b Hendry	1
H.Sutcliffe	st Oldfield b Grimmett	64	c Oldfield b A'beckett	17
W.H.Hammond	not out	119	c & b Ryder	177
D.R.Jardine	lbw b Grimmett	1	c Woodfull b Oxenham	98
E.Hendren	b Blackie	13	c Bradman b Oxenham	11
A.P.F.Chapman	c A'beckett b Grimmett	39	c Woodfull b Blackie	0
G.Duckworth	c Ryder b Grimmett	5	lbw b Oxenham	1
H.Larwood	b Hendry	3	lbw b Oxenham	5
G.Greary	run out	3	lbw b Grimmett	6
M.W.Tate	b Grimmett	2	lbw b Oxenham	47
J.C.White	c Ryder b Grimmett	0	not out	4
Extras	(B3,LB7,W1)	11	(B6,LB10)	16
Total		334		383

AUSTRALIA

W.M.Woodfull	c Duckworth b Tate	1	c Geary b White	30
A.A.Jackson	lbw b White	164	c Duckworth b Geary	36
H.L.Hendry	c Duckworth b Larwood	2	c Tate b White	5
A.F.Kippax	b White	3	c Hendren b White	51
J.S.Ryder	lbw b White	63	c & b White	87
D.G.Bradman	c Larwood bTate	40	run out	58
E.L.A'Beckett	b White	36	c Hammond b White	21
R.K.Oxenham	c Chapman b White	35	c Chapman b White	12
W.A.Oldfield	b Tate	32	not out	15
C.V.Grimmett	b Tate	4	c Tate b White	9
D.D.J.Blackie	not out	3	c Larwood b White	0
Extras	(LB5,W1)	6	(B9,LB3)	12
Total		369		336

		O	M	R	W	O	M	R	W
ENGLAND	Larwood	37	6	92	1	20	4	60	0
	Tate	42	10	77	4	37	9	75	0
	White	60	16	130	5	64.5	21	126	8
	Geary	12	3	32	0	16	2	42	1
	Hammond	9	1	32	0	14	3	21	0
AUSTRALIA	A'Beckett	31	8	44	0	27	9	41	1
	Hendry	31	14	49	2	28	11	56	1
	Grimmett	52.1	12	102	5	52	15	117	1
	Oxenham	34	14	51	0	47.4	21	67	4
	Blackie	29	6	57	1	39	11	70	2
	Ryder	5	1	20	1	5	1	13	1
	Kippax					2	0	3	0

Australia V England —— Feb 18-21 1929, Adelaide.
England won by 12 runs, White takes 13 wickets..

TEST VICTORY DRAMA.

WHITE AND HAMMOND THE VITAL FACTORS.

BRADMAN'S FATAL RUN-OUT

SOMERSET CAPTAIN AS HISTORY MAKER.

Amid scenes of tremendous excitement, England at Adelaide yesterday just beat Australia in the fourth Test match by twelve runs.

The match provided England with far the hardest struggle of the tour. In actual fact, they came perilously close to losing their unbeaten record, for all the time that Bradman, the brilliant New South Wales colt, was in England's chances were poor.

Bradman, aged 20, and batting with the skill and calm of a Test veteran, was run out when in his fifties as a result of a blunder by Oldfield, a fine return by Hobbs, and brilliant bit of work by Duckworth.

From that point, the tables were turned, and Australia had to fight with their backs to the wall.

The splendid batting of Hammond and Jardine were on the one hand great factors in the English win, but even more remarkable, if possible, was the work of White, who in a temperature averaging close on 100 degrees in the shade sent down in the whole match 125 overs, 27 of which were maidens, for 256 runs and 13 wickets.

Considering the conditions, it was the most wonderful performance for a bowler of his type ever recorded, and once and for all ranks the Somerset captain as one of the greatest bowlers of his style the game has brought forth.

The victory of the visitors, although most disappointing to all Australians, was splendidly received by the crowd, who gave them a great ovation as they walked back to the pavilion, White coming in for a great reception.

England's Test Victory, as reported in the Daily Telegraph.

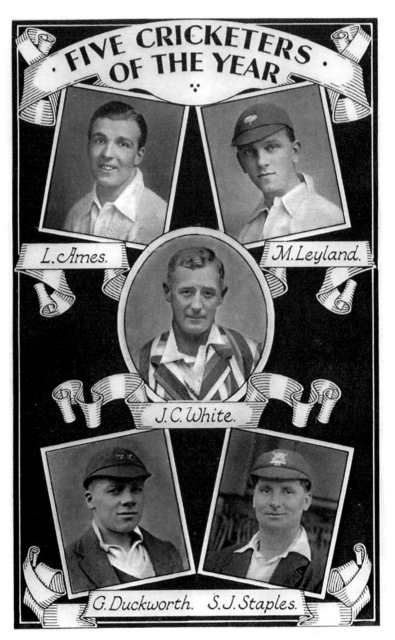

Wisden 1929.

JC White and HG Deane tossing before the England V South Africa test match 1929 at Edgbaston, Birmingham.

JC White's Off Side Field.

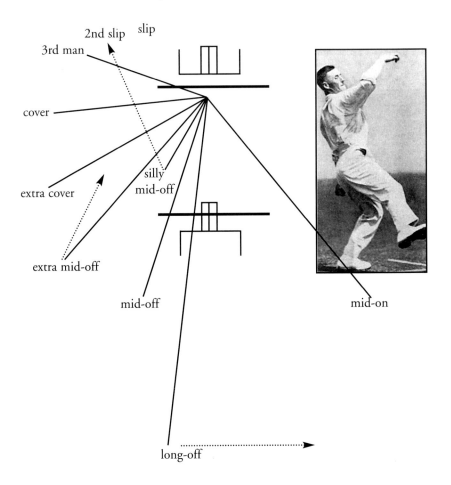

2nd slip slip
3rd man
cover
extra cover
extra mid-off
silly mid-off
mid-off
mid-on
long-off

a) on a fast, true wicket. Note no fielder anywhere on the leg or on-side, except mid-on. The gap on the leg side was intended by White to entice batsmen to hit against his natural break from leg, and thus offer chances to the off-side fielders. Amongst those who accepted many hot catches at silly mid-off were J Daniell, APF Chapman, and Wellard. White's field was set with great exactitude, and he bowled to it with great accuracy.

b) on a rain affected wicket, responsive to spin, silly mid-off went to second slip; extra mid-off moved in close to extra cover; long-off moved to the on-side of the bowler.

Harold Gimblett (enjoying a rare test appearance opening with Len Hutton), and **Arthur Wellard** (inset) both played alongside JC White in the latter stages of his career.

Somerset C.C.C. Museum.

Somerset Memorabilia.

story of the wife telephoning the ground to speak to her husband, only to be told that he had just gone out to bat and replying *"Oh, I'll hang on then"* was probably more appropriate to Ironside than any other competitor for that particular piece of notoriety.

The first Test went entirely England's way from the moment that Chapman won the toss and elected to bat. England scored 521 and everyone contributed runs. Australia made 122. Bradman, unable to staunch the flow of blood on this his first of many innings to come, made 18. With no worries about time limits, Chapman showed his steely side, and did not enforce the follow-on, but gave his bowlers a rest and batted again, eventually declaring at 348 for 8 and setting Australia 742 to win.

The first Australian innings was so short that Jack White had not even been called upon to bowl. Their second innings started badly when Larwood had Ponsford caught behind, and bad light stopped play with Australia 17 for 1. Overnight it rained, and when play started the sun was shining. It was a "turner". Providence had beamed down on the M.C.C. team, and Jack White in particular. We have not discussed in any detail the skills of White's bowling, nor shall we until later when we can indulge in comparisons with other great bowlers, but suffice it to be said here that there were those who said that he did not spin the ball. Well, could he? There were soon to be some very red faces among those who doubted. He was called up to bowl, after an initial blast by the quick men, and in 6.3 overs, he claimed four wickets for seven runs, including Bradman for a single! Three of the four were caught by Chapman, two in the gulley and one at mid-on. Australia had two absentees, and could muster only 66 runs. One of the absentees was Jack Gregory, who burst into the English dressing room in tears saying, *"Lads, I'm done for"*. He was, cartilage troubles ensured that was his last Test match.

Monty Noble, the Australian captain at the beginning of the century, bemoaned the Australian failure: *"Instead of stepping across the wicket, meeting the ball with the full face of the bat, they retreat, drawing away to leg and try to cut with a cross bat with fatal consequences."* Doesn't sound too good for Test-class batsmen!

By the time of the first Test, England had already played six matches, winning two and drawing four, and they had built up a reputation for being something out of the ordinary. The crowds were flocking to see them, and one Saturday in Sydney witnessed no less than 42,757 spectators. The Australian barrackers had soon got into their stride, and selected their favourite targets. The imperious Jardine was a natural, an amateur, an Establishment man, a public schools and University blue, an apparent aristocrat; he couldn't escape. He didn't like it either, which made it all the more fun. He was nicknamed "Sardine" immediately, and when he was out he had to suffer comments such as, *"Get back in your tin Sardine"*. The effusive Duckworth, with his appeals from behind the stumps was another to gain attention, and his name often brought forth the opportunity for the Aussie crowd to take up the chant of *"Quack, quack. Quack, quack."*

Noble wrote of Harold Larwood that he attacked the stumps more than most bowlers, but that he was not averse to spraying the ball about a bit, including some bumpers which were destined to discomfort the batsmen. He then wrote words which a few years later he would be made to eat, and which he must have regretted dearly, *"However as Larwood is not overfast, such methods should not achieve much success against class batsmen, and in the long run should prove too expensive to be persevered with."* Tell that to those Australians who faced the bodyline attack in 1932/33!

Maurice Tate also had something to say about Larwood after that match. In the first innings Larwood had taken 6 for 32, bowling straight and at off-stump. Tate was convinced that Larwood would have done equally well in the Bodyline series four years later if he (or should we say, Jardine) had adopted similar tactic, instead of "fast leg theory", particularly as Larwood by then was much faster than in 1928/29.

The second Test was played a fortnight later, in mid-December, at Sydney. The prospective New South Wales spectators were wild when it became known that their State hero, Bradman, had been dropped and would be twelfth man. He had not done well in the first Test but neither had anyone else. Australia batted first, but a ball from Larwood broke a bone in Ponsford's left hand which side-lined him for the rest of the series.

This game was notable for other reasons also, including the Kippax incident. The player of that name attempted to turn a ball to leg. His leg was well outside the leg stump, but the ball struck his pad and deflected onto the wicket. White was the bowler and did not appeal, assuming that the unlucky batsman would retire to the pavilion. It was the last ball of the over, and the umpire at the bowler's end walked out to take up his position at square- leg. The English players at the batsman's end of the wicket had crowded round the stumps, and Duckworth made it clear that the ball had not touched him. As the square-leg umpire moved in to take up his position for the next over, he was asked if he saw what had happened. He replied that the ball had rebounded from the batsman's leg on to the wickets. Hearing this, Kippax retired to the pavilion. There was much consternation and debate afterwards, and an inquiry was held, as any appeal for a decision should have been to the bowler's umpire, at least in the first place. The results of the inquiry were never made public.

The second day of the Test was the eve of Jack Hobbs' 46th birthday. Knowing that this was likely to be Hobbs' last tour, the Australians kindly organised a "Bobs for Hobbs" fund. The crowd on that Saturday was a record for the Sydney ground, 58,446. During an interval of the play, Monty Noble presented Hobbs with a wallet full of notes and a boomerang on which was a gold shield with the inscription, *"To John Berry Hobbs on his 46th birthday, from friends and admirers in N. S. W."* Hobbs and Noble then linked arms and walked around the ground whilst the crowd cheered and sang *"For he's a jolly good fellow"*. Ah, that we should witness a little of that old world charm today.

England won the Test by eight wickets, scoring 636 and 16 for 2 to Australia's 253 and 397. Hammond scored 251 in 461 minutes. Jack White was economical with the ball but took no wickets. He did have the distinction of hitting the winning run. No less than 170,109 people watched that Sydney Test. Amazingly, nine days later in Melbourne 262,467 came through the turnstiles. The takings were £22,562, so it was relatively inexpensive in those days for the spectators. At the time, 11.1% of the workforce in Victoria was unemployed. Whether this fact helped boost the number of spectators, or reduced it, is not known. Taking account of the average Australian males's predilection for a good cricket match, particularly when there is a chance that those from the Old Country will have their noses rubbed in the ground, it is doubtful whether it had any effect whatsoever.

The third Test was of extreme importance, as an England win would mean that they retained the Ashes. Bradman was reintroduced to the Australian eleven and two other changes were made to their team. England selected the same team which had won the second Test. It is interesting here to consider the wicket-keepers of the two teams. England's touring party included George Duckworth and Les Ames. Ames was of the same style as Australia's Bertie Oldfield, quiet and efficient. Duckworth was probably the first of a new breed, noisy, extrovert and flamboyant. Where Ames and Oldfield would quickly and quietly position themselves to take a ball, Duckworth would arrive there at the last minute with a swallow dive. Each method equally effective, but so very different. There is no doubt that Ames and Oldfield had the highest regard for each other, not least because they went about their duties in similar fashion and were of a similar character. Oldfield was a devout churchman, nicknamed *"the gentleman in gloves"*. Les Ames, when asked to assess Oldfield, replied quite simply, *"He was the best I ever saw"*. In return, Oldfield commenting on Duckworth's style of going full-length to take a ball said, *"I have noticed that Ames was able to achieve the same result and still retain his poise whilst taking similar bowling"*.

Neither Ames nor Oldfield would want to criticise George Duckworth, they were both too gentlemanly for that. It was simply that his style was not their style.

Now Duckworth was an excellent wicket-keeper, who occasionally scored a few runs, but he would never have classed himself as a batsman. On the other hand Ames was both an excellent stumper and a very good batsman. In his career he was to score 102 first-class centuries, and they began to flow from his bat at a very early age. Born in 1905, he scored 1211 runs in his first full season for Kent in 1927. In 1928 he scored 1919 runs and created a wicket-keeping record by catching 69 and stumping 52 batsmen for a total haul of 121 victims. Poor George Duckworth, unable to compete with Ames in scoring runs, had also had a superb year behind the stumps and, had it not been for Ames, would have had a record himself having been involved in 107 dismissals.

Of course, a wicket-keeper's success has to be related to the bowlers who feed him, and Duckworth supporters will not be slow to point out that Ames was fortunate enough to have Percy Freeman in the Kent side. Indeed the Freeman/Ames combination did account for a great many wickets; but Ames also took wickets from the medium pacers because he often stood up to them. Compare his percentage of total victims who were stumpings in 1928, and you will find it is 43%! That is an unbelievable figure when one considers modern cricket. It does not mean that today's custodians of the stumps are any less able than those of yesterday, simply that the game has changed. Today, much of many games is devoted to seamers and fast men with the wicket-keeper of necessity standing back. Hence his victims are mostly catches from outside edges, and stumpings are a rarity, but a rarity which the public cherishes and applauds with a tear in the eye recalling those halcyon days of long ago, when the spinners plied their trade and the newspapers bore such headlines as my favourite, *"Australia beaten - Locked and Lakered"*.

In 1928/29, in the Test matches, the score was Duckworth 5, Ames 0. Why was Duckworth preferred? Others have puzzled over the same question. There are a number of reasons and I am sure the correct answer is a combination of them all. Firstly Duckworth was Ames' senior to the tune of four and a half years, and at ages of 27 and 22 respectively, when the tour started, that was very significant. Secondly, Percy Freeman, Ames' big Kent partner-in- crime was another who was destined to miss out on all five Tests, and there was no doubt some feeling that there was less point in playing "Laurel" if "Hardy" was on the sidelines. Some people were not yet assured that Ames could take fast bowling, and Larwood was going to be a principal bowler in the attack. England had a veritable wealth of batting, arguably the strongest batting line-up ever of any national side. Reference to Wisden will reveal that in the list of "Englishmen" who have scored the most centuries in their career, five of the six at the top of that list were on tour with M.C.C. in 1928/29. At the very top we have Jack Hobbs, followed by Hammond, Hendren, and Mead. There then appears Geoffrey Boycott, immediately followed by his County predecessor Herbert Sutcliffe. What England would give for just one of that sextet today.

So you see, Les Ames' batting prowess was not essential to that particular team. On other occasions it would win him the nod over his colleague and rival, but in 1928 England were very nicely placed for batsmen, thank you.

But surely Percy Chapman of Kent would vote for Ames of Kent over Duckworth from Lancashire, and Chapman was the captain. Would he? Here we have to consider the touring selection committee and the individuals who made up that committee. They were Chapman, White the vice-captain, Jardine the third of the amateurs, and Hobbs and Tyldesley.

When the batsmen were considered for the first Test, Tyldesley had to admit that his tour to date did not warrant his inclusion. As it was decided to pack the team with batsmen, it meant that there was only one other of the touring party who would be unlucky. It turned out to be Leyland, mainly I suggest because he was the young man newly into the side. The batsmen were thus, Hobbs(Surrey), Sutcliffe(Yorks), Hendren(Middx), Mead(Hants), Jardine(Surrey), Hammond(Gloucs). Chapman(Kent) as captain had to play, and White(Somerset) as vice-captain and one of the few amateurs won his place over Freeman. Larwood(Notts) and Tate(Sussex) were automatically in as opening bowlers.

This left only the wicket-keeping birth to be filled. Well, look at the constitution of the side, only one Northener! One Midlander, and all the rest were Southerners. Whatever their respective abilities, the cards were already stacked against Ames getting the wicket-keeper position. There had to be some justice for the North, and Tyldesley was on the selection committee to point that out, if needed. I doubt that it was needed, the North versus South complex had been an ongoing sore, especially for those in the North, who were convinced that the men at Lord's looked no further than their own back door when selecting teams. Percy Chapman was an ambassador and diplomat. He liked, if possible, to keep everyone happy. He would probably give way on points if it kept the tour and players in harmony. If Ames was chosen, not only Duckworth, but the whole of the North of England would be unhappy. If he chose Duckworth, just Ames and his supporters would be unhappy. It was no contest.

There is a final and crucial point. Ames was a nice guy. He was young, pleased to be on his first tour, and much too pleasant to kick up a fuss. As we have seen, Duckworth was the showman, Ames was efficient and quiet. In later life, he reflected that perhaps he was too self-effacing, and that didn't help to do him justice. He realised that perhaps he should have been more extrovert, but at the time he couldn't see the need. So, once more we have an example of the quiet man losing out to the loud one. Jack Hobbs, Sammy Woods, and other great players had said ten years earlier that good old Ernest Robson, the Somerset all-rounder, should have played for England, but Robson like Ames was a quiet gentleman who was too courteous to bang the drum and demand attention.

So, Duckworth got the nod for the first Test, and thereafter England were unlikely to change significantly a winning team. Unfortunately for Ames, after the Ashes had been won, and particularly in the last Test when Chapman tried to give as many of the touring party as possible a game, Ames had broken a finger. The only two players in the party who played in no Tests were Ames and Freeman, the combination who had and were to wreak havoc on the County grounds all over England!

In case the impression has been to suggest that Duckworth was lucky, which he probably was, it is interesting to reflect that modern wicket-keepers are expected to let everyone know that they are around, that they are a focus of operations on the field, a kind of one-man cheer party, and one suspects a planted distraction to the batsman. George was just the fore-runner of a new breed. In fairness to Duckworth, he is reported to have had a very good series, and Ames himself in an autobiography stated that he could not get into the team because George played so well.

Whilst discussing the wicket-keeping protagonists of this series, it would be criminal to omit Robertson-Glasgow's little cameo of Oldfield. He may have been quiet in his actions, but that is not to say that his tongue did not chatter. R-G writes, *"There was a genius of apology in his work as if he, and not you, had made the mistake; and how sociable was that meeting at the crease! He was like a dentist who seeks to obliterate the paraphernalia of action by conversation; on politics, the latest book, or the state of the family's health. He held short tryst with each batsman as he came to the wicket with an airy intimacy peculiarly his own. Some of the nastiest bowling in the world was to be faced in a few seconds; but, first, the little talk. The response was almost universal. Of a few batsmen Oldfield says: 'They would confine themselves to 'yes' or 'no' or 'maybe'; but mostly they caught the idea, and it is reported that once Hendren, during a prolonged taking of guard, discussed his West Indies experiences and the Test match just waited."*

There were only nine days between the second and third Tests and one country game was played in this interim period. Thus, since the first Test there had been no first-class games for members of the touring party to push their claims for inclusion in the Test side. The winning combination of the second Test was retained.

Australia again won the toss but started badly, losing their openers with only fifteen on the board. They then battled their way to a 397 total, with hundreds for Kippax and Ryder and Bradman scored 79. Bradman was not acclaimed for this innings because of his slowness on a perfect batting wicket. Indeed only 168 runs were scored on the second day, 47 of these by England, and it was the lowest number recorded in a full day's Test cricket. Some say that it heralded the type of cricket which would be seen all too often in the future. The critics were forgetting that it was a match which Australia could not afford to lose, and there was no time limit on it. They possibly also failed to take account of the fact that the Australians could not afford to take any liberties with Jack White and his bewildering slow left-armers. He bowled 57 overs and conceded only 64 runs. He took only one wicket, but his marathon allowed the fast bowlers to bowl in short bursts and take the wickets. It is alleged that Bradman's innings was the slowest of his career. Such games bring their own amusements, of course. During the slowest of the play at one match on the Sydney ground, a spectator shouted *"Put Bettington on"*. Soon afterwards he shouted *"Put Bradman on"*. This call was answered immediately from the far side of the ground, *"Put the clock on"*.

England gained a twenty run first innings advantage, mainly due to a second successive double-century by Wally Hammond, who was having the tour of his life. In the Australian second innings, White again bowled a marathon, but this time he also picked up five wickets, finishing with an analysis of 5 for 107 off 56.5 overs. Don Bradman scored 112 and became the youngest Australian Test cricketer to score a "ton", a record he was to retain for only one month, as young Archie Jackson would then make 164 in his first Test. The Australian total was 351. That night it rained, and the pundits were forecasting that England wouldn't make a hundred. Patsy Hendren recalled the occasion, and said that in his experience, there was not a worse wicket in the world than Melbourne after it has been affected by rain and sun. The interesting point was that it not only suited the spinners, as most wickets do in such circumstances, but it became treacherous facing the quick men because the ball had a tendency to stand straight up after pitching. This phenomenon was quickly demonstrated in the match when Bertie Oldfield conceded twenty byes in the first few overs. He just couldn't reach them. Hobbs and Sutcliffe were seen at their very best and gave England an excellent start, the latter eventually scoring 135.

Hendren provides us with a piece of inside information on that game. As the opening partnership developed, Hobbs was not just thinking about his batting, and he came to realise that this was just the type of wicket which his team-mate Jardine would "enjoy". On the pretext of changing his bat, his wise counsel was conveyed to the pavilion and the captain. Chapman was not the sort of person to ignore advice from such as Hobbs, and promoted Jardine to no. 3 in the batting order. Patsy also recalled the tension in the English dressing room. All the players knew how difficult the pitch was in those first two or three hours, and how important a good start would be. He remembered Harold Larwood wanting to go for a walk, but being sharply told to sit down, as there was a feeling that if anybody moved a wicket would fall. The openers saw their side through that hazardous spell, surely one of their finest stands together, and substantial contributions from several of the others meant that England were home by three wickets and the Ashes were secure.

Monty Noble wrote, *"White showed tenacity of purpose and great stamina; our batsmen foolishly permitted him to keep down runs for long periods, thus resting Tate and Larwood for fresh offences"*.

For the first time in the history of cricket England had beaten Australia in the first three Tests of a series in Australia. Percy Chapman had led England in seven Tests and won them all.

There was nearly a month before the fourth Test and England travelled to Tasmania where they won two matches, and then they played a draw with South Australia. Chapman was the toast wherever he went, and he modestly enjoyed his popularity. He never refused an invitation of which there were many. He had become accustomed to having a drink with his lunch, and he continued that practice in the Test matches. W. H. Ferguson, the scorer and baggage man, stated that the only time he saw Chapman lose his temper was when his lunch drink was not awaiting him when he came off the field during the fourth Test.

8.

THE FINEST HOURS

THE FOURTH TEST at Adelaide started on the 1st February. It was hot, but not as hot as when England played there in 1998 and the thermometer rose to 130 degrees Fahrenheit! It is noteworthy that the attendance for the whole match was 137,447, who paid £12,435. That is an average of nearly 20,000 spectators each day for the seven days of the game. In 1998, the first day of the corresponding match, scheduled for five days, attracted 13,600, and a fair proportion of those went home to watch in the comfort of their air-conditioning when live play commenced on television. I do not have the figures for the takings at the 1998 match, but shall we hazard a guess of half a million pounds, and that is excluding the lucrative TV and other sponsoring contracts.

England selected the same eleven as that which had won the second and third Tests. Australia, with nothing now to lose, and following the young Bradman's success, decided to introduce to the Test match arena a second prodigy, Archie Jackson, who was only nineteen years and 152 days of age.

For a change, Chapman won the toss and elected to bat on a wicket which was expected to be a batsman's paradise. In fact there had been a fair amount of rain in the preceding three or four days, and the wicket proved slower than expected. Hobbs and Sutcliffe got off to one of their perfect starts, hardly putting a foot wrong, until Hobbs was out with 143 on the board. Almost immediately his erstwhile partner was stumped off Grimmett when he advanced down the pitch and missed. Soon Jardine was gone and England were 149 for 3 - a mini-collapse. You see, they did happen in those days also. Though not quite as often as seems the case in the late nineties. At the end of the first day, England had reached 246 for 5, but with the prolific Hammond still at the crease.

The second day saw the continuation of the England innings with the obvious plan that Hammond should try to farm the bowling and the others were simply there to keep up an end whilst Hammond established a respectable England total. Australia countered this tactic by bowling outside Hammond's legs and curbing his usual straight and off-driving. Seldom did Hammond attempt to hook or pull, and therefore the Australians could claim to have achieved their ends by keeping the run-rate down. At intervals wickets fell, and when Jack White came to the wicket as last man, Hammond was still three short of his century. White assisted him in reaching that milestone, and when he was eventually caught for nought, Hammond had carried his bat to the tune of 119, taking England's total to 334.

The Australians had another embarrassing start, losing Woodfull to Tate, Hendry to Larwood, and when White came on for an over to allow Tate to change ends, he immediately sent one through Kippax's gate, and the score read 19 for 3. The new boy Jackson played marvellously well for the remainder of the day supported by his skipper, Ryder. Hendren and White were brilliant in the field and Percy Chapman made some astonishing stops, but the Australian pair ruled the roost.

Sunday was a rest day and the Monday morning revealed a different Jackson. Gone was the confident young man of yesterday, to be replaced by a hesitant novice who scored only 20 runs in the hour and a half before lunch. Ryder had started positively, but had been undone when he tried a tactic which had been successful on the Saturday evening, a pulled drive to mid-wicket off White. He failed to make contact and was lbw. Bradman joined Jackson, the two young prodigies together, both out of sorts and lucky to have survived a series of mis-hits. They were still together at lunch when Jackson had 97 out of a total of 201.

Jackson dispatched Larwood's first ball after lunch for four to give him his century and to deprive Bradman of his record of the youngest batsman to make a hundred in a Test. It was as though all Jackson's cares fell away, and he reverted to his exciting and accomplished play of Saturday evening. The same could not be said of Bradman who soon edged Larwood into the slips. Eventually, the ubiquitous White disposed of Jackson, the latter misjudging the flight as he tried to force the ball and falling lbw. He had made 164 in his first Test innings.

England bowled and fielded with renewed vigour after Jackson had gone, and eventually restricted the Australian lead to 35 on the first innings. P.G.H. Fender, writing for an English newspaper, stated, *"White went on imperturbably, and seemed to be the one great strength for England during this period.* (This refers to when Jackson was batting at his best) *Never flurried or worried in any way, either by what the batsmen did to him or by the occasional misfield which, here and there, gave a few more runs than ought to have been given, for the shot made.*" This was, of course, typical of the poker-playing Jack White. They couldn't read his hand and they couldn't read his mind.

 Before the fourth day was very old England were fighting for their lives. For once, both openers failed, and were back in the pavilion before the first innings deficit had been erased. Jardine joined Hammond. Was it possible that Hammond could score well yet again; he had contributed so many runs in the series. They slowly forced the total upwards, and strangely the Australians did not try the leg-side theory on Hammond as they had in the first innings. This was probably because they knew that it was merely a containing tactic, not one which was likely to bring about his dismissal. They felt that they were now in a strong position and Hammond's wicket was what they needed. At the end of the fourth day, Hammond and Jardine were both still occupying the crease, and the England total was 206 for 2.

There had been two noteworthy incidents on the fourth day. After the tea interval, Ryder opened with his faster bowlers, and a new ball. In England, this would not have been allowed. If a ball is damaged so that it cannot be used, it is replaced with a ball of similar usage. In Australia, at that time, a new ball was introduced, and the opportunities for dubious practice are obvious. Fortunately for England, Australia did not have a bowler sufficiently fast to take advantage of the situation.

The second incident occurred when Grimmett was bowling to Hammond. He gave a return catch but Grimmett ran into Jardine's arm, and what appeared to have been an easy opportunity fell to the ground. Grimmett was livid and said to the umpire, *"He did that on purpose."* George Hele, the umpire, took no action. Later, when the players left the field, Grimmett was surrounded by press men, and repeated that Jardine had obstructed him on purpose. When asked if he had appealed, he had to admit that he had not. When Hele was asked about the incident, he simply stated that there had been no appeal. What the outcome would have been had there been an appeal is mere conjecture. The point is that after the incident, Hammond scored a further hundred runs, which turned out to be extremely important.

The fifth day commenced with Hammond and Jardine realising that their job was not yet finished. They added only 55 runs in the hour and a half before lunch. Soon after lunch Jardine was caught at silly-point attempting to drive. He was just two runs short of his first Test century, but he had done an excellent job in sharing a partnership of 262 with Hammond, a record at that time for the third wicket in Tests. With a lead of 247 and only three wickets down, the smart money was on England, but a middle-order collapse was about to materialise. Yes, they had them in those days too, nothing is new. Hendren made only eleven before he was caught in the deep by Bradman. The same situation had arisen in the first innings but Bradman had dropped the catch. This time he miscalculated what should have been a routine catch, and caught the ball high over his head. The crowd thought it brilliant, but those with experience knew that he had nearly made a hash of it. When summing up the series, more than one Australian pressman was critical about Bradman's outfielding, but of course they were unanimous in lauding his batting.

Chapman went for nought, and was soon followed by Duckworth for one and Larwood for five. The Australians were now concentrating on preventing Hammond from keeping the strike. Hammond was dog-tired. He had been on the field of play for the whole of the five days of play with the exception of the first two and a half hours when Hobbs and Sutcliffe were forging the opening partnership on the first morning. When Hobbs was out on that first day, Hammond had gone in to bat. He had then carried his bat through the England innings, being not out. He had fielded throughout the Australian innings; and had returned to the field in Hendry's first over of England's second innings when Hobbs was out. Most of the time the temperature had been in excess of 100 degrees. He was entitled to be tired.

Percy Fender, watching the game with the eye of an expert, noticed that Hammond scored the great majority of his runs with drives off the back foot, his stock-in-trade. He refused to hook and seldom pulled, scoring most of his leg-side runs with leg-glances. Although normally Hammond's favourite shots were the cover and straight drives, his repertoire included all the shots in the book, and one wonders whether he limited himself to his favourites to conserve energy and avoid risk. Patsy Hendren, although failing on this occasion, was a great believer that a batsman should not play certain shots (however much he enjoyed the thrill of them) in important matches because there was too much risk attached to them.

Eventually, Hammond fell, for 177, a personal average for the match of 296! Geary followed, and England's last pair were at the crease, the lead was barely 300. Would it be sufficient? Maurice Tate decided he had better improve the odds a little. Whilst Jack White defended at one end, Tate "hit" at the other. In 50 balls, he scored 47 runs. In desperation, Ryder claimed the new ball, but Tate and White, if anything, seemed more comfortable than against the spinners. As soon as Ryder reverted to his spinners, Tate was lbw, but the England lead was now 348. The tail had wagged, and J.C. had played his part.

The Australians scored 24 without loss that evening, and the next morning England opened with Larwood and White. Larwood had been complaining about a sore foot and often in this match had to resort to bowling medium pace off a shortened run-up. Geary injured a muscle in his leg on the second day, when he had to retire from the field, and had not been fully fit since; and Tate had tweaked his back on the previous evening and bowled throughout the Australian second innings in a great deal of discomfort. Thus, England's strike-force was not at its best, to say the least. Indeed, Hammond was to bowl almost as many overs as Larwood and Geary in the second innings. The England tactic was to keep White going at one end, bowling into the wind, whilst the remainder operated in short bursts with the wind. The pitch was still docile, giving little to the bowlers, but there was a spot just outside the line of the leg-stump of the right-hander.

Jack White hit this spot in each of his first two overs, and on each occasion the ball turned viciously, caught the outside edge of Jackson's bat and flew just wide of Hammond at slip. A second slip was introduced, but the opportunity had gone.

The score passed the fifty mark, and Jackson then hoisted White high over mid-on for four. The field remained the same, and two balls later, Jackson went for the same shot, but White had tossed this one a little higher and Jackson didn't quite get to the pitch. The ball shot off the edge and, tantalisingly for England, dropped between Jardine and Larwood at mid-off and cover respectively. White's countenance did not alter. He liked a batsman to chance his arm, each ball he bowled looked the same but was slightly different. On this occasion the batsman had taken the bait but the bowler had not landed the fish. At the end of the over, Woodfull went down the wicket to caution young Mr. Jackson. Whether he was correct in so doing, we shall never know. There were certainly those at the end of the series who felt that the Australians had been too timid when facing White, and that they should have taken the fight to him much more. The problem was that on this particular tour the scorebooks were full of the disastrous results of batsmen who had tried that alternative.

Jackson did not last much longer, but it was Geary who persuaded him to nick one to Duckworth. Six runs later, White hit the spot once more, the ball jumped alarmingly, Woodfull got a touch, and second slip gratefully took the catch. In the first over after lunch, Hendry was deceived by White's flight and sent an easy catch to Tate at mid-on. This brought Ryder, the Australian captain, to the crease. Percy Fender, watching from the press box, thought Chapman should have put Larwood on for two or three really fast overs, but Chapman persevered with White and tried Geary from the other end. It soon became obvious that Geary's injury was affecting his bowling which was wild and erratic, requiring Duckworth to perform some of his very best acrobatics.

Just before tea, Ryder tried to turn White to leg, was deceived by the flight, and got a leading edge, from which the ball gently looped up and back to Jack White. White, who had been singled out for praise for his fielding and catching throughout the tour, famous for his *"caught and bowled"* in the shires of England, unaccountably muffed it. Percy Fender wrote that it was the first culpable catching mistake made by an English fielder throughout the series, and that it testified to the marvellous work they had done that it should be the second innings of the fourth Test before it happened.

White, poker-faced as ever, simply took the ball and prepared to bowl again. Inside, his stomach must have been in torment. He worked and worked and worked for those opportunities, and he was unused to not accepting them when they came.

The tea interval came and went. Larwood, Tate and Geary, in varying stages of disability, kept one end going, but it was becoming fairly obvious that they were not worrying the batsmen unduly. White had bowled for most of the day, certainly since lunch-time, without change. Kippax was content to simply play him back down the wicket, attempting nothing more extravagant. Ryder occasionally got him away to leg, but Sutcliffe was always deep to prevent anything more than a single. Boundaries had become something of the past. The fourth wicket pair eventually reached their century partnership, and what seemed an age later Kippax reached his fifty. It is doubtful whether he had worked harder for a half-century in his career.

Whether Kippax relaxed a little on reaching the fifty mark, or whether he momentarily lost concentration, we shall never know. He seemed to think he should celebrate in some way, and how better than by hitting White to the boundary with one of his favourite off-drives, which he had denied himself for what seemed an eternity. Up to the wicket came White, over came his arm, and Kippax went for his drive. Almost as soon as he played the shot, he knew that the ball was one of those which weren't quite there for the drive. He was committed and went through with the shot, the ball found a thin outside edge and went very quickly to Geary at second slip. He juggled with it once, and as he fell over he juggled with it again. Suddenly, from first slip, a hand shot out and relieved him of his struggle. Patsy Hendren had come to his rescue, and Geary was very grateful. That ball was destined for the ground otherwise.

The fourth wicket fell at 211, with Australia still requiring another 138 runs to win. The situation could not have been more even. Thirteen runs later, England had the edge. White struck again. This time it was the man he had unaccountably put down when only 26. White bowled what appeared a relatively innocuous ball - didn't they all - and Ryder had gone after him, hitting him straight back over his head. At least that is what he had intended. There weren't many better fielders to their own bowling than Jack White, and for someone to try it on twice on the same day, that was just too much. He caught the ball left-handed high above his head with what must have been razor-sharp reflexes. Ryder had played a captain's innings and scored 87.

The England bowlers, by now, were very tired, and were looking forward to the end of the day, and then to return fresh on the morrow to finish the job. A'Beckett had joined Bradman and they tried to push the score along knowing the bowlers were tired. Chapman consulted Jack Hobbs once more. He had kept White going at the cathedral end, almost as much out of necessity as desire. He would have loved to have given him a little breather. *"What do you think Jack, shall I give J.C. a rest?"* *"No"*, came the answer, as it had on previous occasions when the same question had been put to him, *"Let him keep going."* Jack Hobbs had not become the best batsman in the world without knowing when a bowler should or should not be bowling. Moreover, he had faced White on numerous occasions, and knew that firstly he would be economy itself and secondly that he had the Indian sign over the Aussie batsmen. They both knew that Jack White frequently bowled long periods for Somerset, often throughout the opposition's innings. Mind you, the temperatures were usually somewhat lower than was being experienced in the stifling cauldron of the Adelaide ground. White and the other bowlers had changed their sweat-soaked shirts on more than one occasion, and the intervals had provided them with the opportunity of long draughts of cooling liquid to quench their thirsts and re-hydrate their bodies. Afterwards, White stated that he had a few whisky and sodas during the course of the innings to help him on his way.

Percy Fender wrote: *"White as usual - perhaps I ought to say as always - was bowling on and on at the other end. Occasionally now he was dropping the ball a trifle short, but really bowling a very good length under the circumstances."*

Just before the close of play, White hit the spot once more and the ball shot through before A'Beckett could withdraw his bat. Hammond, only three yards away at second slip, went full length and triumphantly held the ball aloft in his left hand. Oxenham arrived at the crease with two overs of the sixth day left, and Hendren, who had saved many runs with his superb fielding, invested one of them to allow Oxenham to run two rather than one, thereby ensuring that he had to face White again. The ruse did not work, however, and at the close of play Australia were 260 for 6; there were now 89 runs separating the contestants. It was a good game, and even though Don Bradman was still to make his name in cricketing history, there were those who thought that he could see Australia through to victory.

England had stuck to their task all day, and to be fair so had Australia. England had fielded superbly, and Hendren had converted a number of prospective twos into singles by his trick of pretending to pick up the ball when in fact he was still several yards from it. Duckworth had fully justified his selection by a series of marvellous takes down the leg-side off the weary fast bowlers, thereby saving many byes. Fender's assessment of the day was that great catching, allied with White's pertinacity and the really good ground fielding of the team as a whole, were the reasons why England were so well placed.

The seventh and last day of the match was still hot and sticky, but the wind had freshened and came from a quarter which appeared to hinder the England bowlers rather than assist them. Geary and Tate were not fully fit and the former did not bowl. Larwood bowled two or three fast overs but Bradman seemed to take to these and he soon had to be taken off because the runs were coming too fast. Hammond was as economical as any of the quicker men. The Australians adopted a plan against White which at first was quite fruitful. As a left-arm bowler who turned the ball away from the right-hander, he had a strong offside field, and usually employed only two or three men on the leg-side. One of these was usually at mid-on or long-on and one at mid-wicket. There was then a long arc on the leg-side bare of fielders except a forward short-leg, another catching position. White very seldom changed his field from that which he considered was right for the circumstances. He never placed fielders to cover the bad ball. He didn't bowl many. But even if he was hit into the open spaces, he knew that the batsman was taking a chance and would hopefully soon pay the penalty.

Bradman and Oxenham started to come across their wickets and glance White for ones or twos down to fine leg. Chapman had a dilemma. He didn't want to remove one of the two slips because their catching on the previous day had been so fruitful. White varied his bowling from round to over the wicket, but the runs still came. Chapman, presumably with White's connivance, then cut off that run source by moving Tate at forward short leg to backward short leg. It wasn't the best move because the run leakage continued, but now the batsmen were able to push the ball through the forward short-leg position, a much less hazardous shot than going across the wicket and glancing to fine leg. In the stands Percy Fender, and no doubt many more England supporters, squirmed in their seats. He wanted to run onto the field and tell Chapman to restore the forward short leg.

The score slowly rose and at one o'clock, the deficit was down to 41. White's obstinacy then paid off. It was the old bowler/silly mid-off combination which was White's trademark, firstly with John Daniell at Somerset and more recently with Percy Chapman and England. Oxenham came forward and played strongly for the covers. He failed to keep the ball on the deck and Chapman swooped low to his right and a large hand took the catch inches off the ground. Until that moment the match had looked lost to England, now all was back in the balance.

Fender still worried about the run leakage through forward short leg, and his concern was illustrated when Oldfield pushed forward to his very first ball. It trickled only a few yards but was worth a run. The tension around the stadium was now at fever pitch. Soon, however, Fender's concern was relieved as tragedy struck the Australians. Oldfield played a ball into the covers, straight towards Hobbs. He called for a run and Bradman responded. It was suicidal, and Bradman never stood a chance of making his ground. Eight wickets down and 29 needed to win.

Several overs passed, most of them maidens, but the occasional single, often through forward short-leg, reduced the deficit. The situation suddenly got to Grimmett and he heaved at White, trying to pull him through mid-wicket. Grimmett missed and the ball hit Duckworth's pads, so close to the off-stump was the ball that he thought it had hit it and made no attempt to gather the ball. Even Jack White's poker face grimaced, whilst Duckworth's was a study of amazed disbelief. It was lunch-time, two wickets were standing and 23 runs were required for victory!

Percy Fender remembered two things about that lunch interval. Firstly, the excitement was so high that many stalwarts forgot all about the needs of the inner man and simply talked and waited excitedly for the play to resume. Secondly, when play did resume, the forward short leg was back in position, albeit much squarer than previously. Tate, who occupied the position, fielded the ball no fewer than five times in three overs, saving what would have been somewhere between five and ten runs. Tate was now sharing the bowling with White, an excellent move for a crisis situation. He bowled with fire but also to contain the batsmen, and five maidens did he bowl on the trot. His accomplice Duckworth dealt ably with the odd wild ball by performing acrobatics of memorable proportions. At the other end it was the indefatigable White. In he came again, and again, and again. Each ball the same but different. Was the difference actual or was it simply in the batsman's mind? To the ordinary man in the street they all looked as though they could be hit out of sight. The cricketer's eye, if studiously applied, could see that one would be thrown a little higher, one would be a little quicker, one would be held back slightly or dip alarmingly at the end of its flight. In truth, every ball was similar but different. To the casual observer they were all the same; to the seasoned professional batsman they were all different.

White bowled again. It was a trifle short - or was it? Grimmett thought so and tried to become a hero. He went for the square-leg boundary. Unfortunately for him, that was the line where Tate was positioned, and at the second attempt he held on to a stinging catch. In the Chapman household, it had been brilliant captaincy moving Tate to that position. In the Grimmett household, it had been rank bad luck to hole out in a position which until a few overs previously had been vacant. In the White household, old poker-face simply permitted the flicker of a smile and then returned to business. No high-fives in those days!

Thirteen to get, and out to the wicket came Blackie, a left-hander. Poor Percy Fender now had another worry. All tail-enders are leg-side players, Blackie was left-handed and would be pulling with the spin against White, an easier proposition than against it. As Blackie passed Hendren on the way to the wicket, a little psychology was applied. *"I wouldn't be in your shoes for all the tea in China,"* said Patsy. Quite harmless, compared with what might be said today, if all the reports on sledging are to be believed. "Rockerty", as Blackie was nick-named, took his guard. He played forward to the remaining four balls of the over as competently as any of his predecessors had done in their stint at the wicket.

The crowd hoped that Oldfield, one of their favourites, could make inroads into the deficit in the next over from Tate, but Tate bowled a very good maiden, including preventing Oldfield from taking a single at the end of the over and thus retaining the strike. White wiped away the sweat and steadied himself for his 65th over of the innings, twenty-one of which had been maidens. Again Blackie played as though to the manner born. Four times he pushed the ball back down the pitch. The problem was that old poker-face could keep this up all day. Indeed, he had kept it up all day. White bowled again. It seemed a little short. Perhaps it was. It didn't matter, Rockerty had made up his mind, muck or nettles, he was going for this one. He hit it hard, but unfortunately for him and the whole of Australia, it went upwards rather than directly to the boundary. Larwood had been positioned for such a miscue, but he still had to run some distance, about two-thirds of the way to the boundary, before he could catch the ball, and immediately conceal it deep inside his trouser pocket. Pandemonium broke loose as the crowd cheered and the players scrambled for stumps and bails. Hendren fell over Blackie, and feared that to his dying day Blackie thought that he had held him down whilst his team-mates secured the trophies.

England left the field with "Farmer" White pushed to the fore. It had been one of the closest Tests of all time, right to the last ball. The England team had demonstrated what could be achieved by all-round teamwork. Hammond had played two superb innings to set up the victory, but nobody denied that old poker-face, Jack White, had held most of the trumps and taken most of the tricks and applied the coup de grace. During the course of the match he had bowled 124.5 overs, 37 of which were maidens, and had taken 13 wickets for 256 runs. The Test created a record attendance for Adelaide Oval of 137,447 spectators. They paid £12,435 for the privilege.

On the evening after the Adelaide Test, the England party immediately had to take the train to Victoria where they were scheduled to play a two-day game against the gold-rush town of Ballarat. On the train journey, the quiet, modest Jack White was performing handstands. It is amazing how victory revitalises. Had the team lost that Test, the players with little doubt would have been slumped in their seats exhausted.

9.

CONQUERING HERO

PERCY CHAPMAN had become as popular as a cricketing Englishman is able in Australia, but it is awfully difficult to keep all of the people happy all the time. At Ballarat a special arrangement was agreed, as they often were in the country matches, and Ballarat were allowed to have thirteen batsmen against England's eleven. Chapman took the opportunity of resting his Test bowlers - but not White you will note - after the exertions of the previous seven days, and brought into the side all the tourists who had not played in the Test. Fortunately England won the toss and opted to bat, thus giving further respite to most of those who had sweltered in the heat of Adelaide. The temperature was again around the 100 degree mark. England amassed a large total of 493 for 9, with Ames 127 and Tyldesley 65 putting on 100 in 70 minutes at one stage. Jardine came in to bat at no. 11! The home side collapsed in their first innings with seven of them failing to trouble the scorer. In that innings, Percy Freeman had bowled, but in the second innings Chapman used his batsmen as bowlers, no doubt thinking that it would make a better game. Much as the Australian crowd appreciated Hobbs, Hendren and Ames as batsmen, they were not amused to see them doing the bowling. Their dignity was offended, and there were cries of *"shame"* and similar barracking. Chapman had miscalculated in his public relations role for one of the few times on the tour. The incident showed another side of Chapman, a certain obstinacy, because he persisted using his batsmen as bowlers even though it was annoying the crowd.

In the next game the tourists were playing New South Wales in Sydney. On the morning of the first day there was a tropical downpour and a notice was posted to indicate that play would not be possible until after three o'clock. It looked as though play might be abandoned for the day altogether. Several of the England team decided to go to the races. A message came through to the racecourse at 2.30pm to say that play would commence at 2.45pm. The racecourse was some distance from the cricket ground, and the five truants eventually arrived back some twenty minutes late. Chapman won the toss and put New South Wales into bat. Whether this was as a lesson to the culprits is not known, but England started the game short of fielders and with Tich Freeman keeping wicket. The crowd was not amused and the Australian press gave the tourists some stick in their morning editions.

The last game before the final Test was the return game against Victoria at Melbourne. The home side scored 572 with Woodfull reaching 275 not out. Long tiring days in the hot sun was not ideal preparation for the Test.

Percy Chapman did not play in the final Test and there is still a mystery surrounding that decision. Some said that he had been suffering from 'flu, others that he dropped out to give those who had not played in the earlier Tests a game, whilst many thought that he had become disillusioned with his own form and did not rate himself worthy of a place. Whatever the reason, he did not play and Jack White captained the side. He performed his first task perfectly by winning the toss.

The Australians had brought into their side a fast bowler called Wall, but he did not prosper at first as England piled on the runs, with Hobbs 142, Hendren 95, and Leyland, playing his first Test of the tour, scoring 137, in a total of 519. When Leyland returned to the dressing room he discovered that he had been relieved of his gold wristwatch and his wallet containing £65 (a considerable sum of money in those days). The crowd soon became wise to what had happened, and demonstrated their sportmanship by arranging a collection which almost equalled the lost amount.

England were less happy when Australia finished their first innings as they were only 28 runs adrift. This was another timeless Test and the scoring rates on both sides were very slow. The England second innings was off to a bad start when Jardine was out without scoring. He had deputised as opener for Sutcliffe in the match as the latter was nursing a bad arm. Jardine immediately departed to catch the boat for Bombay where he had business to attend to. This action did not endear him to the Australian public or their press. England scored 257 and, after a long slow innings, Australia were home for victory with five wickets to spare. Wall's second innings return of 5 for 66 had been crucial. Incidentally, Bradman scored another century. Hobbs' century made him the oldest man to score such in Test cricket history. White took only two wickets in 75 overs at a cost of 136 runs. Geary was the most successful of the England bowlers with 6 for 136. In one innings, he bowled no less than 81 overs, a record at the time and possibly may be today.

Some thought that England had missed Chapman's captaincy. It is perhaps more likely that they missed him in the field where he was an inspiration to all, and picked up several vital catches at important junctures of the various games. Noble thought that White captained the side well on the two occasions that he had watched him. He wrote, *"I hold also a very high opinion of his capacity as a leader. He captained England in the last Test and also against an Australian eleven at Sydney and made a most favourable impression. He managed his bowlers with discretion, with an eye always on proper contrasts to achieve the best results, and he placed his field with intelligence and uncommon skill. Australians will look forward with keen anticipation to his next visit to the land of the Southern Cross in 1932, perhaps in an even more responsible position than on the present occasion."*

The last sentence emphasises Noble's admiration for White, when it is remembered that England at that time had in Percy Chapman, not only a hero of considerable proportion, but also one who was still in his twenties and therefore presumably available for 1932 and one or two more tours even after that.

The team bade Chapman farewell at Melbourne. He was bound for New Zealand, his wife being the sister of Tom Lowry, the famous Kiwi cricketer and son of a wealthy farmer. Tom and Percy had been bosom pals since days at Cambridge together. Chapman waved his goodbyes with tears in his eyes. He was a genuine man who enjoyed the company of others, and to whom friendships meant a great deal. He had welded a team by affection, enthusiasm and example.

As the cross-continental express roared its way to Perth to deliver the tourists to the final stages of their Australian experience and then to the boat for home, country folk gathered at the wayside stations to glimpse the conquerors and to throw a few well-intentioned jibes. *"Who won the last Test?"*, they would chorus. Back went George Duckworth's reply, *"Who won the first four?"* That journey took four days and four nights. A final match was played at Perth, and that was followed by the traditional football match against the press men. Then, all aboard the "Ormonde" for the long sea journey home. Victoria station was packed with enthusiastic well-wishers several weeks later to greet home the conquering heroes. It was the saturday of the FA Cup Final and most of the team accepted the Football Association's invitation to watch the match between Bolton Wanderers and Portsmouth. At lunch they met the South African cricketers, who had just arrived for their English tour of 1929.

An unbelievable 1,290,420 people had watched the England games in Australia and the gate receipts were £107,947. The M.C.C. as backers of the tour grossed £40,427. The tour had been a huge financial success and a huge social success.

The home-coming of Jack White to Somerset was a day of rejoicing, a memorial to his outstanding feats in Australia. His wife and elder son John had travelled to London to join the welcoming party at Victoria station. At Taunton a civic reception awaited the hero. The mayor of Taunton, Councillor Checkley Barker, was at the station with other dignitaries to accord J.C. an official welcome. Shortly before one o'clock, the main approach to the station and every vantage point adjoining was crowded in anticipation of the arrival. A section of the platform had been reserved for the reception party, which included family members, and in particular J.C.'s children and his father, the latter having been responsible for the whole affair in a manner of speaking by offering to look after his son's farm whilst he was away winning the Ashes. After greetings and hugs and handshakes, the whole party processed on foot to St. Andrew's Hall at Rowbarton, cheered all the way by enthusiastic onlookers. Schoolboys had given up their dinner hour to see their hero, men threw their hats in the air and ladies waved flags and handkerchiefs. The pavements were packed, some leaned out of upstairs windows, others perched on walls or even rooftops. It was a day fit for a royal occasion or the visit of a prime minister, but on this particular day a much more important celebrity was being applauded - Somerset's farmer cricketer, the scourge of the Aussies, good old Jack White.

The banqueting hall was appropriately decorated, and J.C. and Mrs. White sat on the right-hand side of the mayor. Many local celebrities were present including cricketing colleagues, past and present. Sammy Woods was there, doubtless entertaining with his fund of anecdotes. John Daniell was present, the former County captain who had skippered Jack White in his early years, and whose close-in catching had so much helped to augment J.C.'s wicket-taking. There was Guy Earle, a predecessor of Arthur Wellard in the field of six-hitting. Mr.W.E. Maynard of the Borough Restaurant provided the fair, fit for a king.

Following the repast came the speeches. Firstly the mayor himself, proposing the toast of "Our Guest". He had prepared well and appeared to know by heart all of the cricketing statistics of J.C.'s Australian tour. His theme was that they were hosting the finest bowler in all of England, and who was going to argue with him on that occasion. Certainly, the statistics of the Australian tour were impressive enough to support his motion. Jack White had taken the most wickets in one innings, he had taken the most wickets in one Test match, and he had taken the most wickets in the Test series. Further, he had taken the most wickets on the tour, and had the best average, 65 wickets at an average of 22.16 runs per wicket. Apparently, he had also bowled the most overs (734) on the tour, the highest number of maidens (223), the highest number of overs in one match (124) and the most maidens in one Test (50). Jack White did well to achieve all of that, and the mayor did well to have all of those facts at his finger tips. Incidentally, there was one bowling "most" he did not achieve, and that was the most overs in a Test innings. That honour went to Geary who bowled 81 overs in the first innings of the last Test.

The mayor pointed out that cricket was a team game, as did J.C. in his reply, and he emphasised that J.C. could not have achieved his successes had he not been backed up by splendid fielding from the whole of the team. Here the mayor showed that he was not a cricket supporter merely for the day, but that his interest extended to the coming season by expressing his wish that the Somerset team would give the same fielding support to Jack White in the forthcoming campaign. There had been matches the previous year when the Somerset fielding had been described as less than good, and the memories obviously still rankled somewhat with the mayor.

The toast was followed by much applause and the singing of *"For he's a jolly good fellow"*. When J.C. rose to reply the tumult prevented him from starting for fully two minutes. He then spoke generously of the Australian hospitality, the comradeship of the team, and how grateful he was to have experienced the trip of a lifetime.

The only other speaker was Sir Dennis Boles Bart., C.B.E., M.F.H. of *"Up a bit Boles"* fame, when Robertson-Glasgow was playing in his first country house match at Bishop's Lydeard.

If the welcome in Taunton had been enthusiastic; it was matched, though by smaller numbers of people, as the hero approached his home at Stogumber. When the car in which they were travelling was a mile from home, it was brought to a stop by the villagers. They tied ropes to the front of the car and pulled it for the remainder of the journey to Yarde Farm. There then followed more merry-making, brief speeches (country folk don't like anything too expansive), and more eating and drinking. The farm staff presented the gaffer with a tobacco pouch bearing an inscribed silver plate, to which they had all contributed. "Farmer" White was very touched by this gesture and thanked them for making his tour possible by helping his father to keep the farm running. Tom White, in an amusing aside, said that he was not totally looking forward to the morrow when he would have to explain to his son why he had received fifteen shillings a quarter less for his barley than in the previous year.

Jack White was interviewed a number of times on his return from Australia, and therefore some of his comments on the state of cricket at that time are available to us. It was a period when the bat was generally considered to have the ascendancy over the ball, and various changes were being mooted to make the game more exciting. Generally White's opinion was to not meddle, but as a bowler he had some sympathy for making the target a little larger. Two years later, in 1931, the height and breadth of the wickets were increased from 27ins. and 8ins. to 28ins. and 9 ins. respectively. The previous increase had been in 1823. The 1931 increase was extremely significant and needs to be taken into account when comparisons are being made of both bowlers and batsmen over a long period.

There have been other changes which make such comparisons academic, notably the ball. The original laws simply stated that it should weigh between five and six ounces. In 1774, the weight had to be not less than 5. five ounces and not more than five and three quarter ounces, whilst the circumference was to be within the limits of 9 and 9.5ins. In 1927, to assist bowlers, the circumference was reduced to within the limits of 8.8125 and 9ins. Sir Donald Bradman played with both balls and remarked that he was surprised how much smaller the later ball felt. He considered that it was easier to grip the smaller ball, but queried whether the same weight in a smaller sphere would be so conducive to deceptive flight by spin bowlers. Apparently, the great Australian leg-spinner Clarrie Grimmett always expressed a preference for the larger ball.

The lbw rule was under scrutiny at the time (isn't it always), and apparently one consideration was to allow lbw for a ball which had actually snicked the bat but which had not been diverted from its original course. That would have been a tester for the umpires!

Commenting on bowling in Australia, White said that at times he found the bright light rather trying. Couple that with the heat and he found himself much more tired after a day's bowling than would be the case in England. At times he wondered whether he would ever get his arm over again. Well, poker-face Jack never let the Australians know that!

"I was not the only bowler to find that the best policy was to bowl on the off-stump, for with the pitches so hard and the ball turning so little, Australian batsmen are able time after time to turn balls to leg which pitch on the leg or middle stump. One has to bowl what in England would be just short of a length, and they often step back and crack the ball back at you at a terrific pace. It is hard to tempt the Australians to have a go. Jack Ryder clouted me at times and in the last Test Bradman scored on the on-side, but nobody hit me for six, a thing I have frequently to put up with in England. Australia have several youngsters coming on, but of course it is all a matter of doubt as to how they will fare on English wickets, where the ball does more tricks than it does in Australia."

White was reluctant to pick out players from the tour, but he did acknowledge that Hammond had a superb series, as the statistics confirm. He also selected Maurice Tate for special mention as having bowled uncommonly well on several occasions, not always with the luck he deserved. He praised him as a great-hearted trier, who deserved more wickets than he actually took.

White did not contribute to the opinion that more all-rounders were required in English cricket. He preferred specialists. *"Give me the man,"* he said, *"who is good at his particular job."*

In summary of the 1928/29 tour and the part which "Farmer" White played, we can do no better than turn to the experts who were on the spot. Monty Noble, the ex-Australian captain who featured strongly in Test matches at the turn of the century, wrote a book on the series. The following are not the words of a cricket-writing hack who hardly knows the difference between a leg-break and an off-break, they are those of an Australian who is regarded as one of the best ever, and who has seen and played with the best, an uncompromising shrewd cricket commentator.

Noble states: *"In writing of White elsewhere in this volume I have made reference to his extraordinary success as a bowler on Australian wickets. Here I should like to say that it was he, above all, who retained England's hold upon the Ashes. Never have I seen a bowler so consistently overawe his opponents and gradually wear them out by methods that looked so simple. So effective were his tactics, and yet so unostentatiously were they put into execution, that, in the long series of matches played, the batsmen never learned to play him with any degree of confidence, and, as the figures for the tour indicate, he simply imposed his mentality upon them to such an extent that the majority were impotent against him. Apart from his cricket, too, everybody liked him for his quiet demeanour and his fairness. He rarely appealed without being answered in the affirmative. His personality radiated good-will, his gentlemanly and courteous manner captivated all with whom he came into contact, and many were heard to express the thought: 'Here we have a splendid sample of what a great cricketer should be, a true type of English gentleman.' In his own quiet way he became exceedingly popular, and, without being aware of it, made numerous friends. Australia has benefited in many ways by his visit."*

That is some tribute. Jack White must have made quite an impression on Monty Noble, and apparently on the Australian public also. The words about his personality are particularly interesting and will be borne in mind for when we come to consider that side of his character a little later.

Noble continued his appreciation of J.C. by referring to the colossal amount of work which he was called upon to perform, and which he tackled with a smile on his face and without demur. The smile takes some believing, but perhaps the Australian climate was good for J.C. and away from England he could forget his farming worries. Alternatively, perhaps it was a fixed smile, as he said to himself, *"Now what shall I serve up to you, cock."*

Noble maintains that he never bowled even indifferently, was always difficult, and never failed his skipper. *"I admired him greatly as a bowler; I also appreciated his work in the field. Wherever he was stationed he was always on his toes, and chased the leather to the last ditch. He was, indeed, an object lesson and a stimulus to his team-mates as well as to his Australian opponents. I hold also a very high opinion of his capacity as a leader, and Australians will look forward to his next visit in 1932."*

Of course, he never did return in 1932, due no doubt to the rise of Hedley Verity amongst other matters. It would have been interesting to see how he would have fared, and how he would have reacted to the bodyline debate. He could be a hard man, in spite of what Monty Noble says, and I would have expected him to have supported Jardine, firstly as a matter of duty, and secondly because he would expect to give no quarter and to receive no quarter, but I may be very wrong, he had old-fashioned values and he may have thought Jardine's tactics a little infra dig.

Statistics and facts from the tour reveal that England played 24 matches, winning 10, drawing 13, and losing just one. In the Tests, England scored at a rate of almost 50 runs per hour whilst Australia scored at nearly 46 runs per hour.

Hammond led the batting averages for the tour with an aggregate of 1553 runs from 18 innings and a highest score of 251 and an average of 91.35. Six batsmen had averages in excess of 50.

White led the bowling averages with 65 wickets for 1471 runs from 5179 balls at an average of 22.63 runs per wicket. Geary had the next best average with 37 wickets for 25.83 and Tate had the second most wickets at 44 wickets for 30.11 runs.

10.

THE NITTY-GRITTY OF
SLOW LEFT ARM

SO, HOW GOOD was Jack White? How did he compare with the other great slow bowlers, especially the left-handers? All cricket fans have heard of the Yorkshiremen, Wilfred Rhodes and Hedley Verity, even though they played pre-1939/45 war, and in Rhodes' case pre 1914/18 war. Many will remember Johnny Wardle and Phil Edmonds, and of course most recently Phil Tufnell, but these last three are remembered more because they have played relatively recently than because they were great bowlers. Good bowlers, yes. Even very good, but not perhaps to be classed with the likes of Rhodes and Verity. In the "great" category, post-war, we have, arguably, only Derek Underwood.

Jack White of Somerset and Charlie Parker of Gloucestershire were the great left-armers of the years between the wars who are remembered in their counties, and in each others' counties, because they wreaked such havoc on each others' teams, but who will be known only to cricket afficianados of today, not to the general cricketing public. In Parker's case, the reason is not difficult to find. He unaccountably played only once for England. Some rumour seemed to have found its way to Lord's that said Charlie couldn't bowl on a plumb wicket. He was a rather difficult character and so I expect those at headquarters were happy to accept the rumour as fact.

The reasons for J.C. White's lack of recognition are less easy to ascertain. He played for his country on fifteen occasions, including four matches when he was captain. He also played in a number of important representative matches, such as the annual Gentlemen v Players fixture. Apart from his memorable exploits in Australia in 1928/29, he achieved over a hundred wickets a season on no less than fourteen consecutive seasons from 1919 to 1932 inclusive; and in his maturity became a very useful batsman, achieving the double of a hundred wickets and a thousand runs in a season on two occasions. He still lies sixteenth in the Wisden list of most wickets taken in a career, and had a bowling average throughout that career of 18.57. Of the fifteen who have taken more wickets in their career, only six had a better average, and of those six one only was an amateur - W.G. Grace! He captained Somerset from 1927 to 1931, was a Test selector in 1929 and 1930, and became Somerset President in 1961.

His lack of due recognition is probably down to a combination of factors. He played for an unfashionable County, his Test career was limited in England, most of his Tests being abroad, and therefore he did not receive the national exposure which would have accrued had he played a few more games at home. He was a self-effacing man, quiet and not given to the extremes of exhibition, which etch lesser men on the memories of those who were witnesses. He did not seek recognition, he was content just to do his job properly.

If we are going to try to compare "Farmer" White with other great bowlers, we must first define what it was which made him so successful that he could regularly claim a hatful of wickets each English season at such a modest cost in terms of runs per wicket. What was it which made batsmen of renown respect him so much, and which had the Australians in 1928/29 cowering before him.

Firstly, he was a left-arm, usually round the wicket, slow bowler. He had received his early tuition at Taunton School from another slow left-armer, E.J. Tyler, who had performed with great distinction for Somerset at the turn of the century. Tyler was acknowledged throughout the country to know his trade, and Jack White was exceedingly lucky to have not only a professional coach, but more importantly one who excelled in the same type of bowling as J.C. was developing - slow left-arm.

There were those who said that White did not spin the ball a great deal. A remark by White, after his career was over, to a schoolboy sheds some light on that assertion. As he advised him at the school nets, he said that he need not worry too much if he could not spin the ball prodigiously, it was the slight deviation which was important. The bat is only a few inches wide, finding the edge is often sufficient to claim a wicket. It was not that Jack White could not bowl a big break, it was that he chose not to do so. Indeed, there are accounts that occasionally he would break one hugely, just for the fun of it, and on such occasions he would permit himself a large smile.

If one reads the advice of great spin bowlers, they will differ somewhat from each other, but there are aspects of their advice which are always the same. The primary point they make to any prospective exponent of the art is that you must first learn to spin the ball hard. All other considerations and refinements come later. I can't believe that White did not receive the same advice and acknowledge it. For one thing, why do boys become spin bowlers? Because they like to see the ball suddenly changing direction, and be proud of what they can achieve. Oh yes, J.C. could spin the ball alright. It was how he spun it which deserves consideration. There are no motion pictures of him bowling, and therefore we have to rely on photographs, which show us his grip but otherwise tell us little, because we need to know his mode of delivery, the position of his hand when he released the ball, what he did with his fingers prior to delivery, etc. etc. The written word can however tell us a great deal, and we will return to that shortly.

Study of photographs shows that the great Indian left-armer Bishan Bedi had an action remarkably like Jack White's. Bedi was described as poetry in motion, and White's run-up and delivery was not so beautiful or artistic to watch, but the individual elements of their bowling action at the crease were very similar. This is what Bedi said about the art of left-arm spin bowling: *"Learn to spin the ball hard before you do anything else. I remember Jim Laker the England off-spinner telling me that. Try out all manner of grips and arm actions until you know you are spinning the ball and it is turning off the pitch as much as possible. Bowl from as close to the stumps as you can, with your head still. Be natural about the grip. Rest the ball in the fingers, not very tightly nor too loosely. Hold the ball firmly enough to be in control. The index finger and the middle finger are stretched apart, the seam is across, and you simply tweak the wrist in a forward anti-clockwise direction. Pull down and forwards with the index finger. If you simply tug down the index finger across in an anti-clockwise direction you will undercut the ball and it will give you neither bite nor the bounce at the other end."*

Richie Benaud, on the art of leg-spin, states: *"Bear in mind too that it is ideal to create that leg-break with a combination of side-spin and top-spin. All side-spin would mean that the ball will turn a lot but slowly and without a great deal of bounce; all top-spin means that the ball will bounce but not turn from leg."*

Ray Illingworth on off-spin: *"The loop in flight is essential for all good spinners. When flighting the ball I always found that the ball came out over the top of my index finger. The fingers cut less across the ball and more through it, down the pitch towards the batsman. There is as much top-spin on the ball as side-spin. It needs a lot of practice because the arm has got to go through quickly and the ball appear to come out slowly."*

Whenever one reads what his contemporaries thought about J.C.'s bowling, you will find that they attribute his success to length, line, and flight. Also they will remember that he seemed to get much more bounce than most slow bowlers and the ball would come off the pitch quite fast. Bedi, Benaud, and Illingworth, all give the same advice, *"put top-spin into the delivery".* There seems little doubt that Jack White spun the ball as much as the next man, but perhaps he put more effort into the top-spin with less emphasis on the side-spin than most spin bowlers.

He was a great exponent of flighting the ball. The purpose of flighting is, of course, to make the batsman less certain of where the ball will pitch and when it will pitch. The batsman when possible likes to get his front foot to the ball and smother or kill the spin before it can take hold. If he can accomplish this and score at the same time all well and good. Most finger spinners like to see a batsman coming down the wicket. Even if they get tonked once or twice, they know that the batsman is living a little dangerously and giving them a chance. Bishan Bedi writes exactly what I am certain White used to think: *"I used to hate seeing a fine back-foot player at the other end of the pitch because he would go back and wait, create time for himself and do exactly what I wanted him not to do. I wanted him to be coming forward to meet the ball. Then I would look to deceive him in the flight, to make him play at the ball which is landing shorter than he thinks and, when it turns, passes the outside edge of the bat or snicks it. I feel like a fisherman drifting up my bait, waiting for the fish to leap out and make the mistake."*

Of course the top-spinner and its counterpart, the under-spinner, were ideal weapons to counteract the back foot defensive batsman. His ploy allowed the bowler to bowl a fuller length, and then a top-spinner bouncing sharply under his nose or a shooter low onto his legs might well undo his passive resistance.

Jack White always maintained a good length, but what is a good length. The coaching manuals probably advocate something just short of a half-volley, and for the attacking batsman that is perhaps correct. The ball needs to pitch a little short of where it will contact the bat; it then gives the opportunity for it to turn and beat the bat or find its edge, or equally successfully to meet the bat higher up the blade than was intended by the batsman and cause him to play the ball in the air rather than along the ground. If the batsman is going to remain firmly anchored within his crease, a good length will inevitably be further up the pitch; so it can be seen that maintaining a good length does not necessarily mean maintaining the same length. It means bowling the correct length for the particular circumstances

The correct line for an orthodox left-hander will vary depending on the conditions, and various other factors, such as whether a bowler is bowling for containment or has plenty of runs in hand but wickets are needed. On a good wicket, the line is likely to be off-stump or thereabouts. The batsman will be required to play the ball, but unless he is prepared to take a risk by playing against the spin, he will largely be restricted to off-side strokes. This applies to right-handed batsmen only of course.

This brings us to the field settings used by left-handers in general, and Jack White in particular. Firstly, for any slow finger spinner to be really successful he must be aided and abetted by competent and brave close-in fieldsmen. The opportunities of a wicket will often come via the edge of the bat or pad and bat, as the batsman fails to middle the ball or does not get to the pitch of it. The ball may come off the bat relatively slowly or quite quickly, but it will not be in the air for very long, and in those few short moments the fielder must get his hands under it. Now the requirement for a perfect line and length becomes obvious. No fielder likes getting hit with a very hard ball travelling at speed. If the bowler is wayward, he not only gives the batsman increased opportunities to score, he also makes life hell for his close fielders. They will soon be driven from their positions (which it is vital they maintain), or their confidence will be rendered negligible and they will be so worried as to where the next ball is going to land that their concentration on catching will be destroyed. There are a number of very brave short-leg or silly mid-off fielders, but none of them is stupidly so. In his early days Jack White used occasionally to drop one short, and the look he received from captain John Daniell, stationed at silly mid-off or point, needed no words to tell him what he thought of him. From what is written about John Daniell, White HAD to learn to be accurate.

J.C.'s field settings always included the close-in catchers, mostly on the off-side with perhaps one on the leg side at forward short-leg or short mid-wicket. The off-side catchers always included one or two slips, and then one or two in the arc from silly mid-off to gulley. White would never set a field to cope with the bad ball, nor should any bowler worth his salt. His leg-side field was often restricted to just two, a short mid-wicket and a long-on to pick up the straight drives. Often there was an empty space in a large arc from mid-wicket right round to the line of the wickets. Sometimes he would permit a third leg-side fielder in the vicinity of square leg, when it was obvious that the opposition had decided to take risks and pull him from outside off-stump towards the leg-side boundary, but he did this only reluctantly.

The off-side field was built to withstand an onslaught. There were usually four men employed in the arc from mid-off, through deep extra cover, extra cover, to cover point.

Accuracy was perhaps White's ultimate forte; accuracy of line and accuracy of length. How did he achieve that? Unfortunately we can only make an informed assessment. Perhaps not trying to spin the ball too much. A finger spinner has much more control than a wrist spinner, but he still has to avoid over-concentration on the spinning action, reducing his concentration on accuracy of where the ball pitches. It has already been stated that great spin bowlers agree on some aspects of their art but differ on others. It is interesting to recall what some of them concentrated on as they released the ball towards the other end of the wicket. They are very different.

Benaud could not conceive that any bowler would concentrate his mind and his eyes on anything other than the spot on the ground at which he was aiming. He could not understand why a bowler would be looking at the stumps, or worse at the batsman. He suggested that it was probably a "cop-out" on the part of the bowler, saying to himself in effect that it is too difficult looking at the spot where he is intending to land the ball, and instead he is going to land it somewhere vaguely in the region of the ideal spot. Of course Benaud was a leg-break bowler, the most difficult of the spinning arts to achieve with accuracy. He had to concentrate on the spot if he was to be both effective and reasonably economical.

Ray Illingworth, on the other hand, maintains that he never looked at the pitching spot; his eyes were on the batsman! His run-up and delivery had been practiced so many times that he considered that it looked after itself. Why would he want to look at the batsman? For the very good reason of trying to outwit him. He not only tried to read what was in the batsman's mind but he also watched carefully for tell-tale signs. A tightening of the grip on the bat handle, or a slight lurch of the front shoulder, or a twitch of the front foot, might suggest that he was intent upon coming down the wicket to him. Alternatively, a movement of the back foot might indicate that the batsman was about to make space for himself to play out onto the offside. In that case Illingworth would perhaps follow him and direct the ball at or outside the leg stump. A totally different outlook to Benaud's.

Bishan Bedi perhaps came somewhere between the two, though tending towards Richie's theory. He suggests that before you run up to bowl, you must have an exact vision of what you want to bowl at, what response you are expecting from the batsman. On the other hand he states that the batsman he least liked to bowl to was the one who made not a single movement during the run-up, not a flicker of an eyelash until the ball had left the bowler's hand. This suggests that Bedi was at times influenced by what the batsman did, rather than carrying through his own prepared plan. In truth, I expect Benaud would also make a last second adjustment if he noticed something out of the corner of his eye. The Benaud method seems a little safer to the mere mortal than the Illingworth idea. Out-fox the batsman, yes, but to make an adjustment to achieve that in the final second before the ball is delivered must require a very sharp mind.

Eric Hollies, the old Warwickshire leg-spinner, was perhaps one of the most accurate of the leg-break fraternity, but he certainly kept an eye on what the batsman was up to. It is alleged that he was one bowler who made even Dennis Compton struggle. Apparently, as he ran up to bowl; he would watch Compton's feet and made sure that the ball followed them. I expect that was a variation from his normal style specifically to keep the agressive, swash-buckling type of batsman in check.

When you study Hollies' bowling, the secret of his accuracy is partly revealed. Off a brief bustling run, he bowled with a brisk turn of the arm, and his weaponry was mainly top spin, the occasional googly, and leg-spin that was slight but enough to find the edge of the bat. To my mind, he was employing the same aid to accuracy as Jack White - predominance of top-spin over side-spin. Hollies, of course, was the man who ensured that Don Bradman's career Test average fell short of the immortality of 100 by a fraction of a run. Warwickshire had played the Australians a little earlier in the season, and Hollies had dismissed Bradman with his googly. Both Hollies and his captain, Tom Dollery, felt certain that Bradman had not picked the googly, and they were pleasantly surprised when he appeared for a second innings with the Aussies needing only a handful of runs to win. They were convinced that he did so with the express purpose of having another look at Hollies and his googly. Dollery told Hollies not to bowl one. In the Don's final Test at the Oval, Dollery said to Hollies that

Bradman would be looking for the googly first ball. Bowl it second ball. The rest is history, Bradman was clean bowled by the googly. The part I don't understand is, if it was as easy as that, why was Sir Don Bradman the greatest batsman ever, with an average a whisker under 100?

We have departed a little from our assessment of Jack White as a bowler, but having briefly touched upon the success of one "leggie", it gives me the opportunity of diverting for a while to write about an exponent of the opposite art of off-spinning, B.D. "Bomber" Wells. Why would I want to do that? The answer is simple. Cricket interest is stimulated by results and statistics, but the main reason that millions of people around the world follow the game so avidly is the characters who adorn it. Fair enough, but why select "Bomber" Wells from the vast list of those characters? The reason is that I can think of nobody who brings the dreams of the cricketing public nearer to reality. You or I could, with some effort, be a "Bomber" Wells and fulfil the dream of becoming a County cricketer. Bomber Wells looked and was less athletic than most of us. He was a Billy Bunter of a person with spectacles, useless and disinterested at most aspects of the game, but devoted to his bowling. When fielding, he could be relied on, if there was a chase to the ball, to give the batsmen every opportunity to make an all-run four. He was the sort of person you would expect to find behind the pavilion tucking into a large bag of cream buns while the rest were doing press-ups and circuit training. He looked an ordinary person who had found himself, by chance, in a team of professional athletes. He was a character - grand cru - and the more you hear about him the better it gets.

The nickname "Bomber" came from that other Wells, Billy of heavyweight boxing fame, and who banged the gong on the cinema screens during the time of the 1939-45 war prior to the commencement of the next epic film. The only resemblance between the two was their weight, but even there it was distributed around their bodies in a distinctly different manner. "Bomber" played for Gloucestershire and Nottinghamshire, and, before exploring the more amusing aspects of his career, it is only right to say that he was an extremely good off-break bowler. He claimed 998 wickets in his career. It seems so much more appropriate to "Bomber" than 1000 would have been.

Batting used to bore him. How anyone could be bored when they regularly batted for such a short period of time, I do not know. He says, *"I had one stroke, the slog. If I hit it, the ball went a long way and both the crowd and I were happy. If I missed it, well, I was that much nearer to bowling. When*

I batted, I used to run on the sound, as my eyes were usually closed at the moment of impact, and if the shot sounded promising I'd start running." Sam Cook, who had a first class batting average of 5.4 and a top score of 35 not out, was often Wells' partner for the last wicket at Gloucestershire, and the stories of those hilarious partnerships, brief as they were, would fill a book. Cook remembered the occasion when he played a ball and told Bomber to stay where he was. Bomber was standing outside his crease with his bat safely inside. The ball was fielded and thrown in. As it bounced gently along the turf, on a line with Wells' bat, he lifted the bat to allow the ball to pass underneath. The ball promptly hit the wicket and Wells was run out. *"Bloody fool",* said Cook.

There was the occasion when our two heroes came together in a match when Typhoon Tyson was blowing a gale and putting the wind up better batsmen than the intrepid duo. Cook was facing an over from someone of more modest speed, with Tyson steaming nicely, waiting in the wings for the following over. Cook got an edge which evaded the slips and went down to third man, which was unoccupied. Bomber ambled up to the other end to find Sam still there and determined to stay. *"Come on Sam, there's one there."* *"No, I don't think so."* *"There bloody well must be, because I'm standing here talking to you and there's nobody near the ball."* *"Go back, or you'll be run out - again",* said Cook. Bomber walked back bewildered and then the awful truth dawned upon him. It was the last ball of the over and he would have to face Tyson. The first ball from Tyson knocked the bat out of Wells' hands, and the ball looped up towards mid-off. *"Catch it",* shouted Cook, and someone obliged. They were all out. *"Thank God for that",* said Cook, as they all trooped off, *"Let's go and have a beer".*

The most unusual aspect of Bomber's bowling was his run-up. He preferred just one step and then bowl, but captain George Emmett at Gloucester told him he was making the game look silly. Bomber understood the captain's concern and increased his run-up to two strides. Charlie Parker had told him at the beginning of his career that a load of nonsense was talked about run-ups, it was what you did when you got to the wicket that mattered. That was good enough for Bomber, he never believed in taking two steps where one would do. There were occasions when he would bowl without any run-up, much to the consternation of batsmen and umpires alike, and the story of his confrontation with John Langridge is pure folklore. Langridge had been playing cricket for about twenty-five years before he came up against Bomber. Langridge was a man of routine, as some batsmen become, and before facing each ball he liked to complete a programme which included a tweak of the cap, a touch of his abdominal protector, a straightening of the pads, and then a glance up at the bowler before shuffling his feet into position, and then to look at the bowler again. The umpire would have his arm raised throughout this performance, but as soon as he dropped it, Bomber took his one (or two) strides and bowled. This was altogether much too quick a procedure for poor John Langridge, and, his equanimity disturbed, he did not last very long. As Langridge grudgingly withdrew to the pavilion, the umpire apologised. Back came the snapped reply, *"I might have been looking at you, but I wasn't ready!"*

So much for Bomber, he could rattle through an over in no time at all, a much more entertaining prospect than watching a battery of four West Indians bowling about fourteen overs in an hour off thirty yard run-ups. Oh, and one snippet which Bomber received from Charlie Parker, *"Never let a batsman see the top of the ball. Always make him look up at it so that he can't judge its length."*

We must now return to Jack White and our assessment of the attributes which made him successful. He was extremely accurate in both line and length, and bowled with a combination of spins which allowed him to be accurate. One other attribute which he mastered better than most was the ability to flight the ball. His normal line of attack would be at or just outside the off-stump. He could flight the ball so that it came in slightly from the off and dipped. That in itself made life difficult enough for the batsman, but White could vary the amount of spin without any apparent change in his hand, arm and body action. The combination of length, line, and flight, was reinforced by the uncertainty in the mind of the batsman of where the ball would pitch and whether the ball on pitching would bounce high, shoot forward off the ground, turn away, or come on with the arm.

Most slow spin bowlers like a soft, rain-affected pitch where the ball will really bite on pitching. White could certainly bowl on that type of wicket, witness his 4 for 7 from 6.3 overs to finish off the Australians in the first Test at Brisbane in 1928. But he was somewhat unusual in preferring a hard pitch on which to bowl, and the reason was of course that he depended more for success on the other attributes listed above than the sheer ability to turn the ball. Australian wickets, which are normally much firmer than in England, suited him down to the ground.

A.A. Thomson wrote that England was fortunate indeed that Jack White was available to fill the role of left-arm spinner in the years between the great Yorkshire spinners, Wilfred Rhodes and Hedley Verity. How good was Jack White compared to the two Yorkshire immortals, and how did his bowling compare with theirs?

It is very difficult to make judgements for a number of reasons. Firstly, and most importantly, White was an amateur, whilst the other two were professionals. For Rhodes and Verity, cricket was life, almost totally. They depended on it to survive. For White, it was an important and time-consuming passion, but a pastime to be "enjoyed" beside his need to make a living as a farmer. He had to ensure that his time was sensibly divided between the two occupations. Availability of time alone probably meant that the two professionals practiced and honed their skills more than White. For many amateurs, it would have been correct to say that they played the game with more abandon, dash and verve than the professionals could afford to do. The amateurs were playing for fun; the professionals had to protect their living. In that respect, however, Jack White was more like a professional. His attitude to the game was not at all carefree, it was a game to be won. Not that he dwelt unduly on the fact when Somerset lost, and with Somerset's record he could ill-afford to do that, but whilst the game was on he was as canny and dedicated as any professional.

The teams in which they played must have had some bearing on the respective records of the trio. Yorkshire was led, firstly by Lord Hawke and later by others, as a military operation. All of the players, with the exception of the captain and perhaps one other, were professionals, hand-picked from the considerable reservoir of talent which existed in Yorkshire. Each team member was very good. There would not be many dropped catches in that side.

In contrast, Somerset was a financially poor county club which could afford no more than two or three professionals. The majority of the side were amateurs, many were University players, many of them available to play only at certain periods of the summer. It was an ever-changing side, with the emphasis on bonhomie and playing the game rather than winning it. The local papers, and Wisden itself, commented in a number of years that White would have had better analyses if he had received more consistent help in the field.

There are many variations in the playing conditions which must have affected comparisons of individuals. A smaller ball was introduced in 1927, the height and width of the wickets were increased in 1931, the lbw rules have been changed from time to time, etc. etc. The only sensible method to compare individuals is to look at their statistical results, but in so doing, it must be borne in mind that, unless those individuals are exact contemporaries, they will have played under different playing conditions.

The table below gives some idea of the relative achievements of Jack White and four of the greatest, if not the four greatest, slow left-arm English bowlers of the century:

H. Verity (professional) - 1956 wickets at 14.90 av. (1930-1939)
W. Rhodes (professional) - 4187 wickets at 16.71 av. (1898-1930)
J.C. White (amateur) - 2356 wickets at 18.57 av. (1909-1937)
C.W.L. Parker (professional) - 3278 wickets at 19.46 av. (1903-1935)
D.L. Underwood (professional) - 2465 wickets at 20.28 av. (1963-1987)

It will be noted that all are professionals with the exception of White.

Comparisons can be taken further, but are not warranted in the cases of Verity and Underwood, as they could hardly be termed "slow"; they were more inclined to slow-medium bowlers. Comparison with Wilfred Rhodes is interesting. Rhodes was not only one of England's greatest bowlers, he was also a top-class batsman who opened for his country in partnership with Jack Hobbs until the more famous partnership of Hobbs and Sutcliffe came into being. Rhodes scored 39,788 runs at an average 30.80 and was one of the greatest English all-rounders ever.

Rhodes was not a big man, medium height and slim in his early years, though thickening with the passage of time as do many men. His first entry on to the Yorkshire scene was as a bowler to replace the brilliant but wayward Bobby Peel. In his first seasons with Yorkshire he was not at all encouraged to further his batting. It was a Yorkshire custom to protect their bowlers against too much batting which might tire them for their principal task. Lord Hawke would say as Rhodes went out to bat, *"Not more than twenty, Wilfred."* Rhodes always fancied himself as a batsman, and never deviated from his avowed intent to play for England as a batsman. As a young man, his style of bowling was not unlike that of Jack White. He took about four strides, breaking into a trot, and usually appeared round the wicket from behind the umpire. He, like White, was a master of length and line and flighted the ball, but probably spun it more than White.

It was in his attitude to the game that he most resembled White, or perhaps, vice versa. He was a serious individual, not at all light-hearted in his work. In the best Yorkshire tradition, he called a spade a spade, and was totally dedicated to the task in hand, which was either taking wickets or scoring runs. He was not at all like his equally famous colleague from Kirkheaton, George Hirst, who was a very likeable, sociable character, who relaxed and enjoyed himself after work was over. Although they were and are talked about as a duo, they were never close buddies. They respected each other and were friends but their characters were too different for them to be any closer than that. Hirst once said, *"Wilfred isn't a sport."* He didn't mean that he was not a sportsman; he meant that he couldn't let his hair down, have a night out with the boys, and that sort of thing.

Some thought Rhodes rather too dour and his gruff, to the point, comments were sometimes taken to mean that he was a difficult man, which he was not. He was entirely "straight" and expected others to be likewise. He was a very honourable man and had no time for those he did not trust. An example was the Yorkshire secretary of 1920, who was a very able administrator and was later to be knighted for his services to cricket. The occasion related to negotiations of the professionals' payments for certain matches. That year their pay was raised to £11 for home games and £15 for away games, but for the fixtures against Oxford, Cambridge and M.C.C. the rate was kept at £8. This was a bone of contention with the professionals, who argued that it cost them just as much for those away games as the Championship matches. The captain wrote to the secretary and put the professionals' point of view. The secretary replied that he was doing his best to get the discrepancy ironed out. Rumour then had it, however, that Mr. Toone, the secretary, had written to Lord's and told the authorities that nothing need be done about the complaint. Furthermore, the rumour suggested that Toone had stated that it was a Rhodes-inspired attempt to obtain more money. Wilfred never forgot that and never forgave Toone. Even when Toone was knighted he refused to congratulate him upon the award.

The following comments all apply to Wilfred Rhodes. They could easily just as well apply to Jack White. Rhodes was a thinker; he has been described as a professor of cricket. About bowling, he said, *"You don't just turn your arm over, there is such a thing as observation."* He practised his bowling by watching what happened to the ball when he did different things to it. He watched other people if he thought that they had something to offer. His batting is said to have been modelled on that of Sutcliffe, but that must have been later in life, if true, because Sutcliffe was younger than

Rhodes. He also filed away in the back of his mind the details of each player he met. He observed their favourite stroke, and might feed it in the knowledge that they would be likely to play it too often. He noted their weaknesses, not just against his own bowling, but in general. Such knowledge was conveyed at the right moment to his captain, often with profitable results.

This building of a library of the characteristics of players over a period meant that he knew them almost as well as they knew themselves. There is little doubt that Rhodes and White continued to enjoy success when they were beyond the normal retirement age because of their fund of accumulated knowledge of both what they were capable and what others were capable of.

When they bowled they knew exactly where they wanted their fieldsmen, and they could be pedantic about it. Bill Bowes related one such example of Rhodes' insistence. He was positioned at mid-on. *"Go back a bit,"* said Rhodes. He went back. *"Too far,"* said Wilfred. *"Come in a bit."* I came in. *"Now to your right. . . No, too far, come back. . . now in a yard. . . Nay, nay nay!"* Despairing of ever getting Bowes where he wanted him, he marched over, marked a cross in the turf with his spikes, and said, *"See lad, stand theer."* Three balls later the batsman heaved mightily and Bowes managed to get his hands to the catch, otherwise it would have gone straight through him. He was convinced that had he been a yard to the right or left, he would have missed it.

It is a story which should always be told in tandem with that written earlier about John Daniell, who would often get caught in the deep, and return to the pavilion muttering, *"Why can't the bloody fielder stay where his bloody captain put him?"*

Stories abound that Rhodes used to insist on bowling when conditions suited him. Research with his captains demolishes these stories; the nearest one gets is with Lord Hawke, who said that Wilfred sometimes would intimate that the pitch looked right for him. As senior professional he was entitled to make observations, and they weren't restricted to his own bowling. In fact, he was quite reserved with his advice and usually waited until he was asked before it was given. Jack White also received criticism that sometimes he bowled too much. There are two points here; firstly, he was not captain for most of his career and therefore it was in the hands of others whether he bowled or not. Secondly, he was usually having success, which could not be guaranteed if someone replaced him. When tackled once by one of his amateur team-mates, he replied, *"They couldn't hit me, cock, so I couldn't see the point of taking myself off."* "Cock", was the term by which he often addressed people. It wasn't derogatory. It was akin to *"Yes, duck"* used in Lincolnshire, or *"Yes, mate"* used in several counties. Surprisingly, I have never heard *"cock"* used in Somerset, so perhaps it has faded out of use, or else it was a term which was peculiar to Jack White. I have checked on the number of overs he bowled in a season when he was County captain as opposed to when he wasn't captain. I have to admit it was higher. Yes, he did like to bowl!

An area in which White is criticised is with regard to his treatment of the young professionals. It is alleged that he gave them little help and treated them rather brusquely, and there is some justification to this allegation, but it is something to which we will return for further consideration. Rhodes was almost insistent on giving advice to the young professionals of Yorkshire, but I would not mind betting that it was reserved for those he thought would profit from it. He would be unlikely to waste his pearls on someone he considered unworthy of them. Bill Bowes tells another story illustrating both Rhodes' desire to help a young developing player but also to amplify his attention to detail.

Bowes wrote that he and Hedley Verity owed most of what they learned of first-class cricket to Wilfred Rhodes and Emmott Robinson. He recalls that every night the illustrious pair would collect them in the hotel lounge and take them to their bedroom where shaving sticks and other toiletries were pressed into service on the bedspread to represent players, the wicket, etc. etc. These articles were then pushed around the bedspread as their mistakes of the day were discussed and corrected, in detail. He recalls one night when he and Verity had gone to the pictures. On returning, they were assailed by the redoubtable pair, with Wilfred grumbling, *"We'd better get on with it or it will be midnight."* Verity had taken 7 for 26 that day, so Bill assumed that it would be him who would be represented by the shaving brush that evening and who would receive the brunt of attention. Not so, as the toiletries were placed in position, it was undoubtedly Verity's field being depicted on the counterpane. *"Now, Hedley, what did you do today?"* said Emmott. Verity smiled and grew a little and replied, *"Seven for 26, Emmott."* Emmott smote the woodwork at the bottom of the bed in his disgust and made it quiver, *"Aye, 7 for 26, an' it owt a bin 7 for 22! Ah niver seen such bowlin'. Whativver wa't' doin' ta gie A.K. Judd that fower?"* The story goes on but the point has been made. Robinson and Rhodes, in a friendly, fatherly sort of way, were showing the juniors the error of their ways. A good performance was O.K., but if it could be bettered, then it should be. Perfection was what they were seeking.

Jack White was similar to Wilfred Rhodes in many ways. Not only did they both bowl slow left-arm and use accuracy of line, length, and flight to achieve their successes; they were similar in character. They were both rather taciturn, quiet men with subdued personalities. They were serious about their cricket, keen observers, and bowled with their brains as well as their bodies. They were modest men who could be forthright. A smile would cross their lips on occasion and they were not without humour, but extrovert behaviour of any kind was foreign to them. They were dedicated cricketers, one a professional and the other an amateur who would probably have made a very good professional.

Rhodes achieved a high plane in his batting as well as bowling. He was an all-rounder. Only the likes of Botham and Sobers in post-war cricket would rank above him, and even there his bowling figures far outshone them. Jack White was a bowler who learned to bat and who eventually achieved the double in two years running, but in his wildest dreams he would never have called himself an all-rounder. Rhodes was one of the "greats" of cricket, and as a bowler Jack White was not far behind.

11.

YOU CAN'T PLEASE EVERYONE

IN AUSTRALIA, in that winter (or Australian summer) of 1928/29, Jack White had performed the deeds which would register him a place in cricket history. At the ripe age of thirty-nine, he had reached the pinnacle of his career, but it was not to be a fleeting success, for two or three more years he was at the very top of the tree.

In 1929, he had another excellent season with the ball, and also performed handsomely with the bat. Without doubt, 1929 was White's *annus honorabilis*. He led Somerset in the county championship for the third year and skippered England in the first three Test matches against the South Africans, winning one and drawing the other two. In the national bowling averages, he secured fourth place with 168 wickets at an average of a little over fifteen runs per wicket. His batting probably gave him even more satisfaction and he achieved the "double" for the first time in his career. That summer he also made his highest score in first-class cricket - 192 against Nottinghamshire at Taunton, and what a day he chose to achieve it. That was a golden day indeed. The 24th July would long be remembered in the White household, and in those of many fervent Somerset supporters. The majority of the runs had actually been scored on the previous day. His innings had been chanceless and had occupied about five and a quarter hours. It had included twenty-three fours. He was last out when eight short of his double century, caught behind the wicket. The Somerset total had reached 411, one of only three occasions that they were to pass the three hundred and fifty mark that summer.

In the luncheon interval, J.C. was presented by Lord Bath, Lord Lieutenant of the County, with a silver salver and £955 worth of War Stock. (I hope that wasn't the same Stock as my mother inherited and which was hardly worth the value of the paper on which it was printed by 1950). The presentation was from the people of Somerset, in honour of Jack White's performances in Australia. The local paper reports that, *"White looked a handsome, bronzed figure as he stood there in his England blazer, receiving his gifts modestly, as becomes a cricketer, but plainly moved by the emotions of the occasion. Around him were Lionel Palairet, Sammy Woods, John Daniell and others who in their day had given Somerset cricket a glory all its own."*

Having written above about the War Stock, imagine my surprise to read in the newspaper the very next day that it could, at last, after eighty plus years be coming into its own. *"Every well-directed cheque, well loaded and properly pinned, is a more formidable weapon of destruction than a 12in. shell."* David Lloyd George, the Prime Minister, used those words in 1917 to encourage the British people to invest in War Loan Stock to finance the First World War. The Government originally issued £2 billion of war loan gilts - the equivalent of £120 billion today. The interest was initially £5 per £100, but in 1932, in a move often referred to as the *"financial Somme"*, the Government reduced the rate to £3.50. It was a tragedy for investors, who lost a fortune by investing their money in that patriotic vehicle. However, many economists are now predicting that the Stock could soon become attractive. The Stock can be bought at about three quarters of its face value, giving a fixed rate of return of approximately 4.5%. As other interest rates continue to fall, the Stock will become competitive. Hence the old saying that everything comes to he who waits. Unfortunately, most of the original investors are now dead, and even their inheritors can't make a killing because as soon as the Stock starts to pay a rate higher than newly issued gilts, the Government will simply buy in the debt. There is a moral in that little story somewhere. Incidentally, there are also stocks called Consols, which date from the 19th century when they were used to fund the Napoleonic and Boer Wars. A similar situation stands with them.

Let us return to the day when Jack White received his War Stock. On this particular day, Farmer White certainly proved to be the man for the occasion, because he proceeded to claim his hundredth wicket of the season (What timing! His most fervent supporters claimed that he had reduced his wicket intake over the whole of the previous week so that he could save the hundredth for the day of the presentation!). Being White, he didn't content himself with the one wicket, he proceeded to capture six wickets for 91 and gain a first innings lead of 192.

It would be unfair to the Nottinghamshire batsmen not to inform you that they actually hit six sixes off J.C., Bill Voce getting four of them. But batsmen had hit him for six on other occasions, and usually had quickly paid the price for their indiscretions, as did the Notts batsmen.

The large crowd was certainly getting their money's worth on that July day, and the fun continued when it was discovered that the wooden pavilion next to the press box had caught fire. The game was suspended, and the Taunton Volunteer Fire Brigade arrived with commendable dispatch. They spent ten minutes pouring water over the flames (and over themselves, it is reported), and then having done their duty, like true men of Somerset, they stayed to watch the final half-hour's cricket. Oh yes! When they had a good day, they made the most of it in those days.

Another important landmark to Somerset cricket occurred in 1929. Arthur Wellard had completed his two year's registration. This mighty smiter of the ball was let loose on the cricketing public, who adored him, and on the County opposition who treated his arrival with a good deal more circumspection. Wellard is known in history for his batting feats and especially for his six-hitting, but he was principally a bowler, and a very good bowler to boot. In his first season for Somerset he took 131 wickets at an average of little over 21 runs each with his medium-fast out-swing. Somerset should have climbed to a more exalted position in the County Championship, with White and Wellard in harness, but the batting was, to be kind, unreliable. Nevertheless, they were as always good entertainment value. Guy Earle had been a hitter for a season or two when Wellard came on to the scene, and the supporters had glorious dreams of just half-an-hour with these two together at the wicket. Unfortunately it didn't happen often, because neither was inclined to hang around for very long. They executed their business with panache!

The dreamers were rewarded when the old foe, Gloucestershire, came to Taunton, and there was nobody they would like more to see have it *"put up 'em"*. Wellard had a tremendous match, batting at no. 9 he scored 130 and took 11 wickets for less than sixteen runs each. In Somerset's first innings Wellard scored 75 out of a total of 144 and hit two sixes and nine fours. He was obviously playing with caution this particular day. Not to be outdone by this young upstart, who was threatening to depose him as hitter-in-chief, Earle reached his half-century in 15 minutes. It was the old story though, the other batsmen failed to perform and Somerset lost by 64 runs. But what entertainment! I wonder if that was how the supporters looked upon it. Has the need to win always been a part of human nature, and not a recent phenomenon as some would have us believe. Did the fans leave the County ground after that wonderful day's entertainment, saying,

"If only Earle knew when to stop", "Why doesn't he play a more controlled game?", "He ought to get his head down a bit, instead of hitting at everything which is bowled to him."?

Earle was an amateur, he was playing because he enjoyed the game, and he enjoyed the way he played it. If others differed, that was their bad luck. Wellard, as a professional, was in a more vulnerable position. If he hit out and was successful, everyone was happy. If he hit out and failed too often, he was on the scrap-heap looking for a job. It is understandable that some are of the opinion that the demise of the amateur took a little of the carefree excitement out of the game.

Returning to the exploits of J.C. White, we find him playing for M.C.C. versus South Africa in early June. He had a good match and took 5 for 87 off 40.5 overs and 1 for 30 off 16 overs. In his only innings he scored 39. The match was drawn, and the Times correspondent wrote, *"For the greater part, the batting was uninspiring; the bowling, apart from J.C. White, was not unduly difficult."* He must have had a poor lunch, not White, the correspondent.

Later in the month White captained England in the Test trial. The most telling comment in the Times, stated that *"the captains were astute"*.

J.C. was appointed captain of England for the first three Tests against South Africa. In the first Test at Birmingham, Sutcliffe and Hammond scored centuries. White was economical to the tune of only conceding 51 runs off 45 overs, but he did not take wickets. The Times correspondent wrote, *"White's length was, of course, impeccable, but there was no evidence that he was flighting the ball as he can."* The match was drawn.

In the second Test at Lord's, Sutcliffe again scored a century, but the England innings got off to a bad start when they lost their first three wickets for a mere eighteen runs. Patsy Hendren came in, and as the Times put it, demonstrated the worth of an old horse for a bad road. In the South African innings Duckworth had one of those games behind the stumps which he would have been eager to forget. He missed both catches and stumpings. White took 2 wickets for 61 from 35 overs in that first innings. When England batted a second time, White joined Maurice Tate at the wicket and informed him that he was keen to make a declaration and therefore could he hurry if he desired his hundred. Maurice obliged, secured his century, and White, who was 18 not out, declared the innings closed. In the South African second innings, the Times reports that *"White was inspired to bid Robins to change ends and to reintroduce Larwood. Things then began to happen with suddenness and frequency."* However, South Africa held out and the game was drawn.

The third Test was held at Leeds in mid-July. White took 0 for 24 from 17 overs in the first innings and 3 for 40 from 23 overs in the second innings. He also scored 20 not out. England won.

White's record as captain in the series was won 1 and drawn 2 from the 3 matches, but for some reason A.W. Carr was appointed captain for the fourth match. As so often happens, no sooner had the announcement been made, and before the fouth Test commenced, J.C. scored his highest innings in first-class cricket. It was the 24th July when he plundered Nottinghamshire for 192. As he had an excellent bowling return in the same match, the poor Test selectors must have had very red faces.

The Thirties arrived and the pre-war decade would provide resolute cricket with outstanding personalities and drama and intrigue in a concoction of excitement. Bradman blossomed and enjoyed his finest hours. The Australians took the Ashes in England. Jardine retaliated with Larwood and the bodyline series in Australia. Hedley Verity burst upon the international scene, only to have his illustrious career cut short by gunfire in Italy. More professionals were entering the game and the swashbuckling amateurs were becoming fewer.

Down in Somerset in 1930 Jack White had yet another very good season, and for the second year running he achieved the double. His worth as a bowler was now without question, but his shrewdness as a captain had also been noted, and he had the honour to be appointed to the triumvirate of the Test selection panel. Wisden observes, *"Although called away on a few occasions by his duties in connection with the Selection Committee, White took 111 wickets in championship matches for 17 runs apiece and scored nearly 1000 runs. In addition to leading the side with fine judgement, he was the big all-rounder of the eleven and for the twelfth successive season he took over 100 wickets."*

His championship bowling is worthy of further consideration, and illustrates his amazing ability to be both penetrative and economical at the same time. In the County Championship matches he bowled 1117.5 overs for 1961 runs and took 111 wickets. That is an average of only 1.75 runs conceded per over, and an average of 17.66 runs per wicket. The second of those figures alone is outstanding, coupled with the other it is amazing. Penetrative bowlers, i.e. those who have a high return of wickets for the numbers of balls they bowl, also tend to concede more runs per wicket.

They buy their wickets with vicious spin or a variety of differing deliveries. Inevitably they lose a degree of accuracy and are punished for it, but that is their method, and quick wickets at any cost is sometimes quite acceptable to a captain on the attack. Doug Wright, the famous Kent and England leg-spin and googly bowler, would concede well over three runs per over, twice the rate of Farmer White's 1.5. As discussed earlier, White's fortes were line, length, flight and a modicum of spin, but especially forward-spin. Thus there weren't many opportunities for the batsman to score off him because they were tied down by his accuracy. They could use their feet and come down the wicket to catch him on the full, and occasionally someone of the calibre of Bradman did that, but for other than the very best batsman it was a hazardous undertaking, because White was so good at flighting the ball, making it difficult to judge exactly where it would pitch.

Perhaps equally as important as his bowling, it should be noted that even Wisden is now referring to White as an all-rounder. He had certainly improved his batting year by year, until he had become a useful middle-order batsman. Indeed, for Somerset he frequently batted amongst the top five, although that was partly due to some indifferent performances from his colleagues.

He was chosen (as a selector, I suppose he chose himself) to play for the Rest in the England v The Rest Test trial at Lord's, and was the most successful of the Rest's bowlers, taking 3 for 50 off 22 overs. The match was drawn and England batted only once.

White was chosen for the 2nd Test at Lord's, the Test in which Bradman considers he played the finest innings of his career. All of his shots went where he intended and all, with the exception of the one from which he was dismissed, were along the ground. He scored 254 out of a total of 729 for 6 declared. Even in that game, when England were put to the sword, White was the best of the bowlers with 3 wickets for 158 runs off 51 overs, still only three runs an over conceded even in that run glut. His victims were Ponsford, Kippax, and - yes, Bradman, caught by Percy Chapman at extra mid-off. That was to be his last Test against the Aussies. He might easily have gone on the next trip to Australia, with Jardine, but for the emergence of one Hedley Verity. Bradman, great man that he was, had learned to play J.C. and the learning had begun several months before when he had been selected for an Australian XI against England early in the 1928/29 tour. As it happens, White captained the England side that day and they convincingly beat the opposition. Bradman was the one success and he had ground out the slowest fifty of his career, in two and three quarter hours, against a White who gave him nothing.

In Somerset the characters continued to parade their talents, or in some cases lack of them. Seymour Clark achieved an unenviable place in the records when he played five matches, nine innings. I believe he probably hid himself when his time came for the tenth. He registered nine ducks, and it is said that on one occasion Peter Smith of Essex, taking pity, tried to get him off the mark with a bad ball which bounced twice and yorked the hapless Clark on the second bounce. In later years he would dismiss his batting misfortunes by stating that he was actually played for his wicket-keeping! That's the attitude, perky to the end. It reminds me of my elder son who registered a good set of "O" levels, but then seemed to decide that school work was for others. On receiving enquiries concerning the outcome of his "A" level examinations, he would reply, with complete conviction, *"Oh, I passed with ease (E's)"*. It didn't seem to do him any harm either.

Another recruit to the Somerset ranks that year was Bill Andrews, who was to have the distinction of being sacked by Somerset on four occasions, twice as a player and twice as coach. Bill was a larger than life character from Weston-super-mare and lived for cricket even before he met Arthur Wellard, who used to tutor him and his brother in the nets, of an evening before taking them to the pub and winning all their earnings at pontoon and poker.

Bill wrote his autobiography later in life and titled it "The Hand That Bowled Bradman". The incident happened in 1938 and the title of the book does not reveal that Bradman had scored 202! He recalls a host of stories, including the occasion when as a schoolboy he took 6 wickets for 0 runs. After the 5th victim was out, he became so excited that he bowled the next one quickly - the batsmen had crossed in the previous dismissal. He was hit for six but it didn't count because the incoming batsman had not arrived at the wicket!

Bill didn't like Jack White, although he admired him as a cricketer and agreed that he was a superb bowler. Even here he qualifies his praise by adding, *"he should have been, the number of overs he bowled"*. He also claimed that J.C. picked the seam, and that it was a not unusual practice in those days. His comments on White's batting were also congratulatory. He didn't think that he had a vast amount of natural ability, but he had tremendous guts. He recalled seeing him hit on the body time after time by the fast bowlers, but he never saw him flinch for a moment (shades of Brian Close).

He also commended him as a first-rate fielder and field-setter who gave away absolutely nothing. That sounds like Jack White.

Andrews, looking back on his apprenticeship under White - he was his skipper in his first two years - thought that J.C. was probably good for him, but he could not come to terms with the lack of warmth in their relationship. He recalled the occasion in his second match when he made a particularly good diving catch at mid-off to dismiss Reggie Santall off White. J.C. mumbled, *"Well caught"*, and Andrews claims that was the only bit of encouragement he received from him in his first two years.

On the contrary, he claims that he dropped an easy catch off J.C. in the slips in his first County match and was taken out of the position and never returned there for five years. Well, White was captain for two of those years only, so either there was a degree of exaggeration in Bill's allegation or the wrong was not of White's doing. At Nottingham, George Gunn hit a ball like a rocket and Andrews dislocated a finger trying to stop it. The only comment he received from his skipper was that he should have stopped it!

The subject of the experienced established players being remote from their junior counterparts and not giving them sufficient advice and encouragement has arisen a number of times in Somerset's history. The most famous is the case of Viv Richards. When he was not retained by the County, the accusation was made against him, and of course the consequences are infamous with not only Richards and Joel Garner departing the County, but their buddy Ian Botham also. Fortunately the acrimony has been laid to rest and those fine players have made their peace with the County.

Andrews, as coach, makes the same complaint against Bill Alley and Colin McCool, and other overseas stars have been likewise criticised. One would think, in the interest of team spirit and team achievement, advice should be forthcoming from the seniors, but it is probably not as straight-forward as it appears. They are professionals and are paid to perform and produce results, not teach others to achieve the skills which might mean that they replace them in the team. Some of them would argue that their talents are natural and specific to themselves and that they do not have the ability to coach others in text-book style. Cricket is a stressful game, even for the best, perhaps more so for the best as so much more is expected from them. It might be all they can cope with to keep themselves afloat without the added worries of others.

These are arguments, but I have to confess that they do not appear too convincing. Star sportsmen achieve an icon status and regretfully many lose their humility. The Gods are placed there to be worshipped not to administer to the needs of others.

Back to Bill Andrews and some of his stories. His ambition had always been to play for Somerset. He must have been delighted after having a trial to be told that he was "in". In those days it was a pretty precarious "in", and in his case it meant that he would play in the next four matches. That was the only guarantee he had; no wonder his father went wild at him giving up a permanent job to pursue a dream - a dream which might soon turn into a nightmare. He was also told that he would bat at No 11. He recalls that there were five professionals playing, and four of them occupied places 8, 9, 10, and 11. The amateurs had to have a reasonable place in the batting order.

Andrews recalled his first meeting with Larwood. Tom Young, the senior professional for Somerset who opened the batting, made 32, but Andrews noticed that he kept his pads on when he returned to the pavilion after he was out. Being Andrews, he wasn't afraid to enquire the reason. Back came the response, *"It would be a waste of time taking them off. We'll soon be bloody well batting again."* He was right, Somerset lost by an innings and 45. Horace Hazell was Somerset's no. 11 at the time and he could bat a bit. In fact, when he was sent to a winter indoor school in London, he was sent back with the report that he would never make a bowler but his batting had possibilities. In Somerset he was called *"The Crisis King"*. He had sat in the pavilion watching the mayhem as Larwood extracted the utmost venom from the wicket, cracking one man's finger and making the ball fly alarmingly. When it came to his turn, Horace, who had no doubt been hoping that they would give Larwood a rest, departed for the middle humming hesitantly, *"Nearer my God to thee"*. This was the same Hazell, who in partnership with one Bert Hunt, crucified the famous Hedley Verity one day at Bath when Verity's analysis was 89 runs conceded in 9 overs, the highlight (or lowlight for Verity) being 28 from Hazell in one over, which included four sixes.

Bill recalls his penultimate innings for Somerset, when he knew his job was on the line. The game was against Nottinghamshire, and as he arrived at the wicket he asked Arthur Jepson, that prolific Notts quickie, to go easy as it was his last chance to get a contract for the following season. Andrews is convinced that he was plumb lbw, caught right in front of his stumps when he had scored only six, but there was no appeal from Jepson.

A lovely story, well done Arthur.

The best line in Andrews' book comes after he has related story after story, keeping the reader riveted with all these wondrous tales, and he writes, *"I can't be sure how many of these stories are true"*!!! (my exclamation marks, he doesn't have any, just the simple sentence).

Recalling one or two of Andrews' stories reminds me of the Robertson-Glasgow observation on the duties of "the gatesman" (Phew, putting Bill Andrews in such celebrated company as R-G! He would have been highly chuffed with that). The duty of the gatekeeper was to open and close the gate which allowed the players access from the pavilion and enclosure to and from the playing area, usually, but not always, a nice white-painted wicket gate in picket fencing (how appropriate). Robertson-Glasgow recalls how the gatesman subtly varied his approach to this duty, according to who was passing through. Nos. 1 and 2 would be treated with a silent deference and the gate thrown wide open as soon as they appeared on the pavilion steps. Nos. 10 and 11, on the other hand, might receive a comment, nothing to do with cricket (it would be wasted), but if they should happen to glance behind them on the way to the crease, they would see that the gate had been left open!

You can imagine extentions of that story, such as when a batsman had been totally and adamantly unconvinced that he had touched the one which had been caught by the wicket-keeper, or that he had definitely got bat onto the one which thudded into his pads when he was plumb in front. If the recipient of such an "unfair" dismissal happened to be named Gatting or Botham, for example, there is little doubt that the gatesman would quickly open the gate and retire without a murmur, trying to merge with the crowd. Those gatesmen who had to deal with a gate which sported a couple of those spring hinges, which automatically closed the gate if it was not held open, were definitely at a disadvantage in such circumstances.

To make up for such occasions they had their moments of glory, when the press photographers gathered to catch the incoming hero who had just scored a rapid hundred. The photographs were usually taken just outside that little wicket gate, and an experienced gatesman could manoeuvre himself so that he appeared in the ensuing print, just over the right shoulder of the hero. He would ensure, of course, that he wore a suitably serious face, so that his employers would not accuse him of bringing his post into disrepute, but he grew a little when the photograph appeared on the morrow in the Daily Telegraph, though even then he would feign a disinterest when acquaintances excitedly commented on the photograph, and mumble that he could not see what all the fuss was about.

The curious fact about such happenings was that the hero of yesterday was none other than the disenchanted Gatting or Botham of the day before!

In the winter of 1930/31, England toured South Africa and White was one of the chosen tourists. It was a tour which was dogged by ill-luck. Sandham was injured in a motor accident soon after arrival and took no further part in the proceedings. 'Flu affected a number of the team and at times they had difficulty in fielding a full side. Five Tests were played and after South Africa had won the first by 28 runs, the remainder were all drawn. It was a very even series and England were unlucky to lose the rubber. In the second Test, South Africa had an opening partnership of 260 which remained, until recently, their highest in all Tests. In the final Test play was held up for seventy minutes at the beginning because the correct size of bails were unavailable. Apparently the umpires had to make two sets! That seems unbelievable.

Jack White played in four of the Tests and bowled with his usual economy but he bowled only 148 overs in total. His analysis was 148 overs, of which 43 were maidens, and he claimed 10 wickets for 308 runs i.e. an average of 30.80. Bill Voce was the most effective bowler and Ian Peebles had some good matches, which probably accounts for J.C. having less work than usual. White's tally for all matches on the tour was 29 wickets at 24.06 runs per over.

The tour party had sailed to South Africa on the S.S. Edinburgh Castle and we find that Jack White was very much involved with the high jinks on board, leg-pulling and elaborate jokes leading to ingenious counter-measures. On one blazing hot day, as the ship crossed the equator, J.C. had poured a jugfull of ice cubes down the back of one startled girl. Bob Wyatt and Beet Chapman, the popular wife of the England skipper, resolved to make him pay for his dastardly deed. They acquired a dozen hot-water bottles and that night lined the bed with them in White's promenade deck cabin. J.C. 's frenzied attempts to track down the bottles before the air in the cabin became unbreathable were watched by a large and appreciative audience.

Incidentally, I was surprised to discover that there was a touring team to Egypt in 1930, and in the second "Test" the tourists were beaten by 62 runs!

White's Test career had now finished, but he was still a force in the land in the County championship. 1931 season brought him 128 wickets, but for the first time his average topped the twenty mark, 20.36 to be precise, and he headed the Somerset bowling once more. His most memorable games were when he scored 100 at Nottingham in three and a half hours as he tried to stave off defeat, and the match against Sussex at Eastbourne. He took two wickets with consecutive balls in the last over to secure victory and had a second innings analysis of 9 for 71. His match analysis was 13 for 133 in just under 80 overs. The last wicket was his hundredth of the season, and he was bowling with a badly bruised finger.

The close of the season brought the unwelcome news that Farmer White found that he could no longer continue as captain. At 40, although still top of the tree at his bowling and playing as well as he had ever done with his batting, his withdrawal had begun.

Somerset, with Ingle as captain, had their best season for a decade, finishing seventh in the county table, and for the first season for many years they won more games than they lost. An improvement in the batting was largely credited with the revival, but the old captain played his part, though he appeared in only half of the games. Once more and for the last time he claimed over one hundred wickets, and again he featured in the top ten in the country in the bowling averages. He had the great distinction of having taken more than one hundred wickets per season for fourteen consecutive seasons since the First World War, from 1919 to 1932 inclusive. His analysis for 1932 reads 107 wickets for 1813 runs from 978 overs at an average of 16.94 and with a concession rate of only 1.85 an over. His more notable efforts for the year included taking 15 wickets for 96 runs against Glamorgan at Bath. In the second Glamorgan innings he destroyed his chances of notching all ten wickets for the second time in his career when he took a catch off Young, bowling at the other end. Thus he had a hand in all ten wickets.

Jack White continued to play intermittently for four more seasons until he finally called it a day in 1937. He still enjoyed his great days such as the 11 for 136 with which he helped to beat Gloucestershire in 1934, and the two centuries which he scored in 1935. He also witnessed the advent of other Somerset heroes, not least Harold Gimblett, who played his first game for the county in 1935, and what a first game. Almost discarded by the county before he had even played a game, he was a last minute replacement against Essex at Frome. He borrowed Arthur Wellard's spare bat, batted at no. 8, scored his first fifty in 28 minutes, a hundred in 66 minutes, and 123 in 79 minutes. What bliss to have been there! Good old Somerset, once more they had unearthed a treasure - even if they had nearly thrown it back before they realised its worth. As one hero was bidding a fond farewell, another was walking in through the open door.

12.

A MUSEUM OF MEMORIES

SOMERSET C.C.C. continued, after J.C. had bowled his last ball in earnest, in the same loveable fashion, always pressed for cash, forever equating the sublime with the ridiculous. Even after the second big interruption to cricket's progress, in 1939-1945, the county reconvened with only eight professionals. They were supplemented by the usual array of colourful amateurs, and the atmosphere and deeds were much the same as before. They enjoyed their cricket and sometimes it was to their opponents considerable discomfort, as on the occasion when Wellard was not treating Sam Cook of Gloucestershire with the respect which he considered his bowling deserved. As yet another six made its way out of the ground, George Lambert comforted his beleaguered companion with the assurance, *"Don't worry Sam, he's been mis-hitting them so far."*

Somerset also continued its tradition of smiting the mighty and bowing down to the underdog - not that there were too many of the latter around. India toured in 1946 and at Hove they scored 533 for 3! Next match was at Taunton, where they were demolished for 64 and lost by an innings. You could never tell with Somerset just when they were going to be brilliant.

The farce also continued, though perhaps not to the high level it reached in the thirties, when Billy Ashdown, Kent's opening bat, pushed well forward to a ball and was struck on the pad. There was one lone appeal which appeared to come from the direction of extra cover. Ashdown was disappointed, to say the least, to be given out on the optimistic appeal of someone not in the best line of vision for such matters. The position was rather worse than he realised for the appeal had come from Somerset's 12th man, Buttle, watching the proceedings from outside the boundary.

The stories are legion and perhaps that is one of the endearing qualities of cricket. I can't imagine that football or baseball or any other sport can produce a fraction of the stories credited to cricket. And as Bill Andrews said, *"I don't know whether all these stories are true."* Post-war Somerset is not a subject for this book, but there continued to be excitement if not always substantial achievement. The 40's and 50's, in terms of results, were fairly barren years with captains coming and going with some regularity. The 60's were an improvement and the Australian imports began to arrive, mostly for just a season or two, but in Bill Alley's case for evermore. Then came D.B. Close and the swinging 70's; that must have been a shock to the systems of some of those who liked to play the game in a more casual fashion. The culmination was the era of Botham, Richards and Garner, when the spectators enjoyed sweet success in results in addition to hours of excitement and entertainment.

The 90's have been a relative anti-climax, how could they not have been - but hope rests eternal. The senses tingle with excitement in the new millennium. Somerset is bound to have something up its sleeve to celebrate such an occasion. It won't, of course, know what it is; but that is the beauty of it. Glorious uncertainty and wonderful surprise. They will probably thrash the Aussies by an innings at Taunton. Don't tell me that they are not coming to Taunton. That does not matter. That is being too realistic. An element of daydreaming is required, when facts become unimportant, and the impossible becomes only improbable. Put your faith in those who follow those wonderful characters of the past - Woods, Tyler, Palairet, Daniell, Gimblett, Wellard, White. . . . . .

If you do wish to submerge yourself into a world of reverie, you could do worse than pay a visit to the County Cricket Museum, or better still become a £5 per annum member. With loving care, Tony Stedall, supported by Clifford Jiggens and other volunteer helpers, maintain a veritable Aladdin's cave of cricketing memorablia, and it is all housed in the delightful old Priory Barn which stands beside the County ground and dates from the fourteenth century. It is the only building remaining of the Augustinian Priory of St. Peter and St. Paul founded in 1158. "Barn" is somewhat a misnomer as it is thought that the original building served as quarters for guests or lay members of the Priory. The relatively recent restoration of the building to become the cricket museum was financed by the Supporters' Club and cost, together with grants, in the region of a hundred thousand pounds. A library of books, all donated, grows annually and a lending library service is available for members. In addition there is an impressive reference library with a set of Wisdens, County Year books and other rare documents. The body of the barn is rearranged each year and houses display cases, photographs, sets of player cards, mounted balls of meritorious occasions, signed bats, caps and other headgear, scorecards of famous matches, and even a pair of Joel Garner's size fifteen boots.

There is a story, or indeed host of stories, behind each exhibit, and hours delving into the comprehensive library would no doubt reveal many of them. For example, there is a silver cigarette box donated by the late Lord Rippon of the Heath government. It was presented, fully autographed, to his father, A.E.S. Rippon, by the team of the time in 1922 on the occasion of the latter's wedding. The Rippon twins, A.E.S. (Sydney) and A.D.E. (Dudley) first played for Somerset in 1914. They both had a hard time of it in the trenches of the Great War and both were seriously wounded. Sydney was wounded at the first battle of the Somme and meningitis set in. He recovered but the experiences left him highly strung and stories abound of his strange actions, one or two of which we will hear shortly. It was Dudley however who suffered most from his experiences and in early 1920, when he returned to the team, he looked a different man. He opened the innings with his brother, but an unfortunate mix-up resulted in him being run-out without scoring. His nerve went and he could not bring himself to bat in the second innings, and that was the last occasion on which he turned out for the County. Just one example of the horrible after-effects of war.

Sydney and Dudley were look-alike twins and one can imagine the consternation that would cause to scorers and journalists particularly. They often dressed alike which didn't help, but even when they permitted some distinguishing difference, such as different caps, they were not averse to a little horseplay by swapping caps half-way through a match. It is reliably reported that one of them once got three ducks in a schoolboy match, two for himself and one for his brother.

Sydney once caused concern in high places when he played under an assumed name, his grandmother's actually. It eventually transpired that he had done this because he was on sick-leave from the Civil Service and he thought they would be unappreciative if he played cricket whilst on a "sickie". Unfortunately, or fortunately depending how you look at it, Sydney did rather well in the match and scored 92 and 58 not out. The headlines applauding the advent of this newcomer were just what Sydney did not want if he was to hide his misdemeanour from his employers. The outcome was good, however, as the Civil Service showed its right side and accepted the happening without penalty. He was an Old Etonian and it was cricket. Someone from the local elementary school and playing football and the outcome might have been more serious! Just imagine if the truth had never come out, Wisden's immaculately compiled records would have been wrong for all time. I wonder how many hidden secrets their records do conceal.

Sydney was eccentric to say the least, and at the wicket he would twirl the bat like a drum-major's baton. As his score advanced so did his cap, round his head, until the peak was very nearly facing backwards. One of the best Rippon stories must be the occasion when he was 99 not out overnight. He had been batting in new pads and felt that they were too stiff. That evening the hotel guests watched in amazement as he buckled on his pads and proceeded for two hours to run round the corridors until he was satisfied that the pads had been "run in". Next morning he was out first ball!

The display unit in the museum lovingly exhibits the silver cigarette box. The stories behind it have to be earned with reading.

A recent addition to the museum is Ian Botham's bat with which he scored his heroic unbeaten 149 at Headingley in 1981. It had experienced a chequered career since Both had given it to Dennis Breakwell who offered it as a prize item at an auction in aid of Taunton Football Club. It was a heavily taped Duncan Fearnley Magnum and the winner sold it to a Plymouth man, for £330, who allowed his young son to play with it in the back garden. After a dormant period of fifteen years in an attic, it was offered to Lord's for permanent display, but rejected, we know not why. Presumably they could soon become inundated with bats from famous occasions. Eventually the then owner met Mervyn Kitchen by chance and the future of the bat was discussed. Fortunately Mervyn suggested that the museum was a suitable home and there it now stands. Many cricket fans will still remember that glorious day in 1981 when Botham put the Australians to the sword, and I would wager that a little research would spawn a succession of stories that would equal those arising from the silver cigarette box.

Another item of national as well as local importance is the Lawrence Challenge Trophy, presented by Sir William Lawrence, for the quickest century of the season and won in 1935 by the immortal Harold Gimblett, unbelievably and in fairytale fashion in his very first game for the County. I wonder what the attendance was at Frome that day. I can imagine them, aroused by the shouts and applause, tumbling out of the beer tents into the glare of the sunlight and wondering who the hell was this phenomenon, who looked very ordinary but played like a saint, and a Somerset saint to boot. There must have been many Taunton regulars, deprived of the event, who bemoaned missing the occasion to their dying days.

The museum houses a number of tableaux, one commemorating W.T. Greswell (1889-1971), a contemporary and not too distant neighbour of J.C. White in West Somerset. He was reputed to have introduced in-swing bowling, and played a number of good games for Somerset. In 1912 he took 132 wickets at an average of 17.78, also reminiscent of White, and it has often been stated that had he been available to join J.C. in bowling harness after the war, Somerset would have been a team to be reckoned with. Unfortunately for Somerset he spent most of his time in Ceylon, tea-planting, but where he did as much as anyone to promote the emergence of cricket in that sub-continent.

Another tableau is of Taunton School with photographs of the school earlier in the century. I keep meaning to go back to see whether the old walnut tree was still standing at the time. Now it could tell a few stories, little doubt about that.

Soon after Jack White had retired from County cricket he was involved in a shooting accident which cost him the sight of an eye, but he was still very active in encouraging others to play cricket and used to attend Taunton school nets to bowl a little to the boys. His advice was sparing but what he had to say was well worth remembering. He also attended the Stogumber village nets and would sometimes place a half-crown on the stumps to be won by the lad who could bowl him out. He had always enjoyed field sports and was a member of a pheasant and partridge shooting syndicate. For several years he was the secretary of the Quantock Staghounds Hunt.

As a young man he had married a Miss Mortimer, who was a farmer's daughter, and they had four children, two boys John and Tom and two girls Joan and Nora. John was killed in the second world war whilst serving as a Wing Commander in the Mediterranean. The younger son, Tom, who followed his father into farming but who had no great interest in cricket, remembers that his grandfather made cider but his father's favourite tipple was whisky and water. He smoked, as did most men of that era, possibly twenty cigarettes a day. He very much enjoyed his poker, attending a poker school in Taunton weekly, and was a very good player. A number of his cricketing colleagues would have vouched for that and long journeys by train gave them plenty of opportunity to gain unhealthy experience of the fact. He also liked an occasional flutter at the point-to-point races.

Tom remembered Percy Chapman staying with the family and also one or two Australian cricketers, but he was quite young at the time so does not remember their conversations. Tom recalls his father as being very even-tempered, perhaps a little reserved as a family man, presumably no great show of emotions. That does not of course mean that he did not have feelings; it isn't everyone who wears his heart on his sleeve.

J.C. had just reached the allotted three score years and ten when he died. Earlier in the year he had yet another honour bestowed upon him when he was appointed President of the Somerset C.C.C. It was 1961. The committee and the supporters wished to have a fitting memorial to their hero of yesterday, and made the excellent choice of a pair of wrought iron gates to be erected as the main entrance to the County ground at Taunton. The gates have the initials J.C.W. depicted in the scroll-work. The gates were paid for by public subscription and dedicated on May 1st. 1963 at the start of the new season. W. T. Greswell had followed his colleague and contemporary to become president of the club and it was to him that fell the honour of paying tribute to "Farmer" White at the inauguration ceremony. The gates were unlocked by the captain of the club, Harold Stephenson, and J.C.'s widow, Mrs A. White, together with members of the family were the first to pass through. They are now familiarly known to cricketers and supporters as the "J.C.W. 's".

As our story nears its end, it is appropriate to assess Jack White as both a person and as a cricketer. As a person he was not quite everyone's choice of the ideal, but as a cricketer his outstanding talent and achievements are unquestioned and unanimously acknowledged.

Bill Andrews was his greatest critic, and even Bill accepted that J.C. was a brilliant cricketer. Bill found him unhelpful and unappreciative. It is quite understandable when one considers the characters of the two men and the difference in their ages. Bill was a very loud sort of person, never a shrinking violet, even as a newcomer a boisterous, confident young man. When Bill joined Somerset, J.C. was in his early forties. As a young man he had been the exact opposite of Bill. He had been quiet, self-effacing, even a shade lugubrious. You can imagine his reaction to this uppety young puppy, particularly as White was captain. He would determine right from the start that he would bring him down a peg or two, and there is no doubt that he gave Bill Andrews a hard time. He did not handle the situation well. Indeed he made an enemy for life. Andrews was one of the few ex-Somerset cricketers who did not attend J.C.'s funeral. My impression is that J.C. was perhaps a little Jekyll and Hyde in character. Among his amateur compatriots he was light-hearted, a good companion. The professionals, particularly the young ones, needed a firmer hand.

Another critic was J.C.W. MacBryan, who felt that White was over-bowled to the detriment of the other Somerset bowlers. He thought that he was too selfish as a player, though he acknowledged how good a bowler he was, and always had tremendous respect for White as a poker player. Whether MacBryan's criticism of selfishness is justified is open to doubt. White was only occasionally captain when MacBryan was playing, so it was someone else who decided how much of the bowling he did. Also MacBryan was a very good batsman who perhaps did not receive the national recognition he thought he deserved. There may have been a little envy of White's success.

The inimitable John Arlott had the good fortune to see Somerset and Jack White against his own county of Hampshire in the summer of 1929, just after White had played havoc with the Australians. It was only Arlott's eighth first-class match and he was fifteen. Arlott wrote:

"I expected to see terrific spin, but because it was a plumb Southampton wicket White relied on flight and accuracy; the ball rarely turned but he did seem to make it dip in to the bat through the air. Slowly it dawned upon me that though every ball might look the same, the batsmen constantly dealt with one in a different manner from the one before, often hastily changing their stroke to do so. It was probably the most profound cricket lesson I ever learned. Accuracy did not mean that every ball was the same, but that each was of a good length for its pace - and occasionally White bowled a quickish one. I had been watching from in line with the wicket, and briefly I went round to watch from square-on and there could see the varying arcs of flight. It was all such a fresh area of understanding that it remained with me all my life. There was the pace of Arthur Wellard to admire, but the fascinating part of the day was the bowling of John Cornish 'Farmer' White. When play ended that day, spectators came on to the ground and formed an avenue applauding, through which White walked into the pavilion. He had bowled 58 overs - 23 maidens - and taken six wickets for 103. He showed no reaction at all to that applause but many years later I had the opportunity to tell him what an effect that day had on a boy spectator. Sixty years on, that memory is still clear on the mind - and crystallized one boy's first sight of Somerset, of J.C. White, and of what flight in bowling really meant."

R. C. Robertson-Glasgow, in an Appreciation of Jack White, stated:

"On a dusty dry surface, and most of all on a batsman's paradise, there has not been, among modern cricketers, a greater slow left-hand bowler. Jack White was the yeoman four-square. His work on the field, either cricket or farm, was conducted with an unhurried certainty and an unsurprised understanding of natural obstacles. Whether it was cows or batsmen, he had the treatment for the trouble, and he never seemed to tire. In cricket he was serene, but not merely placid, for the artist in him could resent too much luck in an opponent, or too little attention in a fielder. As to the latter he would often say, 'the trouble about that cock is that he's fast asleep.'"

The secret of his bowling could be seen, if never quite understood, only from very close. The spectators and the Press just watched perfection of length, but if you were near the crease you could marvel at the slight but infinite variety of his bowling. He made the ball "do" a little each way on the truest of surfaces without advertisement from his fingers; and he could make the ball jump unexpectedly high even on a wet slow surface, often hitting the splice or near it with the opportunity of a catch to the close-in fielders. Jack despised demonstration, such as arm-whirling at a near miss, and all the nonsense of the mere showmen. For him tomorrow was another day, but he did not lack wit, shrewd and pungent. By observation and industry he rose to become a competent batsman. In defence, he was a believer in pads as well as bat, remarking, *"you know the umpire's often wrong in the right way."*

Patsy Hendren, commenting in later life on White's performances in Australia, said:

"One day in Melbourne Jack White bowled from one o'clock to six o'clock, and I think I can say with conviction that never have I seen a bowler in any one spell retain such a high standard of accuracy. For proof of this I would refer you to the figures. During the whole day the Australians scored only one hundred and sixty runs or so. I know people who would say that it was painfully slow cricket. Judging by the clock it was. But believe me, the real pain was for the batsmen who had to watch every ball with never a one sent down which they could treat with other than the greatest respect."

The Australians, understandably, were very ready to sing J.C.'s praises and we will end the story by hearing from just two of them. C.G.

McCartney stated: *"He placed his field splendidly and bowled to it, and rammed home the lesson that good length is essential to successful bowling."* Joe Darling said, *"How I should have revelled in having such a bowler when I was captaining Australia! He would never have been left out of a Test eleven with me."*

APPENDIX 1

STATISTICAL NOTES

J.C. White was born at Holford, Somerset, on the 19th. February 1891 and died at Combe Florey on the 2nd. May 1961 aged 70 years. He played for Somerset between 1909 and 1937, captained the team from 1927 to 1931, and became president in 1961.

He played fifteen times for England: 1 v Australia in 1921, 1 v West Indies in 1928, 5 v Australia in 1928/29, 3 v South Africa in 1929, 1 v Australia in 1930, and 4 v South Africa in 1930/31.

He captained England on four occasions, including the fifth Test against Australia in 1929 and the first three Tests against South Africa in 1929. He also toured South America with the 1926/27 M.C.C. team and was a Test selector in 1929 and 1930.

He had an aggregate of 2,356 wickets at an average of 18.57 runs per wicket, and scored 12,202 runs at an average of 18.40 including six centuries. He performed the double of 100 wickets and 1000 runs in two successive years in 1929 and 1930. His highest score was 192 against Nottinghamshire in 1929.

His 2,356 wickets lies sixteenth in the Wisden list of career totals of bowlers in England of all time, and only six of those above him had a better average. His average runs per wicket is second in the amateur's list, beaten only by Dr. W.G. Grace.

His 2,167 wickets for Somerset is by far the highest for the county and his average of 18.02 runs per wicket is by far the lowest.

His 381 catches is comfortably the highest career total of all Somerset players.

His notable performances include:

16 wickets in a day against Worcestershire at Bath in 1919, 8 for 36 in the first innings and 8 for 47 in the second innings.

All 10 wickets for 76 runs in an innings against Worcestershire at Worcester in 1921.

A hat-trick against Middlesex at Lord's in 1923.

He took nine wickets in an innings on four occasions:

9 for 46 v Gloucestershire at Bristol in 1914
9 for 58 v Warwickshire at Birmingham in 1922
9 for 71 against Sussex at Eastbourne in 1931
9 for 51 against Glamorgan at Bath in 1932

He took fifteen wickets in a match on three occasions.

With C.C.C. Case he holds the record fifth wicket partnership for Somerset of 235 made against Gloucestershire at Taunton in 1927.

The most notable performance is his achievement of more than a hundred wickets in a season in fourteen consecutive years:

Year	Ovs	Runs	Wkts	Ave
1919	748	1621	102	15.89
1920	1015	2133	137	15.57
1921	1081	2238	139	16.10
1922	1091	2207	146	15.11
1923	1061	2252	147	15.32
1924	1016	2177	144	14.42
1925	1023	2001	121	16.53
1926	1307	2424	127	19.08
1927	1132	2063	112	18.41
1928	1336	2720	138	19.71
1929	1556	2648	168	15.76
1930	1117	1961	111	17.66
1931	1218	2606	128	20.36
1932	978	1813	107	16.94

In most of those years he had an average in the top ten bowlers in the country, his highest position being 2nd in 1929.

His Test record is:

Series	Tests	Ovs	Runs	Wkts	Ave
1921 v Australia	1	36	107	3	35.66
1928 v W.Indies	1	27.3	53	3	17.66
1928/9 v Australia	5	406.4	760	25	30.40
1929 v S.Africa	3	129	187	5	37.40
1930 v Australia	1	53	166	3	55.33
1930/1 v S.Africa	4	148	308	10	30.80

APPENDIX 2

1928/29 AUSTRALIAN TOUR

First Test(Brisbane):
England...... 521 and 342 for eight
Australia..... 122 and 66
England won by 675 runs.

Second Test(Sydney):
England...... 636 and 16 for 2
Australia..... 253 and 397
England won by eight wickets.

Third Test(Melbourne):
England...... 417 and 332 for 7
Australia..... 397 and 351
England won by three wickets.

Fourth Test(Adelaide):
England...... 334 and 383
Australia..... 369 and 336
England won by 12 runs.

Fifth Test(Melbourne):
England...... 519 and 257
Australia..... 491 and 287 for five
Australia won by five wickets.

England scored 3,757 runs for the loss of 87 wickets, giving an average of 43.18, whilst Australia scored 3,069 runs for the loss of 90 wickets and an average of 34.10. (Australia had three instances where a man did not bat through illness or injury).

England's runs were scored at a rate of 49 per hour, and Australia at 45 per hour.

THE TEST MATCH AVERAGES

England Batting:

	Inns	N.o.	H.S.	Runs	Ave
M.Leyland	2	1	137	190	190.00
W.R.Hammond	9	1	251	905	113.12
E.H.Hendren	9	0	169	472	52.44
H.Sutcliffe	7	0	135	355	50.71
J.B.Hobbs	9	0	142	451	50.11
D.R.Jardine	9	1	98	341	42.62
C.P.Mead	2	0	72	80	40.00
E.Tyldesley	2	0	31	52	26.00
A.P.F.Chapman	7	0	50	165	23.57
H.Larwood	8	0	70	173	21.62
M.W.Tate	10	0	54	214	21.40
J.C.White	8	4	29	70	17.50
G.Duckworth	9	4	39	76	15.20
G.Geary	8	1	66	95	13.57

Australia Batting:

	Inns	N.o.	H.S.	Runs	Ave
A.A.Jackson	4	0	164	276	69.00
D.G.Bradman	8	1	123	468	66.85
A.G.Fairfax	1	0	65	65	65.00
J.Ryder	10	1	112	492	54.66
W.M.Woodfull	10	1	111	491	54.55
A.F.Kippax	10	0	100	311	31.10
H.L.Hendry	8	0	112	227	28.37
O.E.Nothling	2	0	44	52	26.00
E.L.a'Beckett	4	0	41	104	26.00
P.M.Hornibrook	2	0	26	44	22.00
W.A.Oldfield	10	2	48	159	19.87
R.K.Oxenham	5	0	39	88	17.60
C.V.Grimmett	9	3	38	95	15.83
T.W.Wall	1	0	9	9	9.00
V.Y.Richardson	4	0	27	35	8.75

D.D.J.Blackie	6	3	11	24	8.00
C.E.Kellaway	1	0	8	8	8.00
W.H.Ponsford	3	1	6	13	6.50
H.Ironmonger	4	0	4	5	1.25

England Bowling (6 ball overs)

	Ovs	Mdns	Runs	Wkts	Ave
G.Geary	240.3	70	477	19	25.05
J.C.White	406.1	134	760	25	30.40
H.Larwood	259.1	41	728	18	40.44
M.W.Tate	371	122	693	17	40.76
W.R.Hammond	169	30	287	5	57.40
D.R.Jardine	1	0	10	0	-
M.Leyland	3	0	11	0	-

Australia Bowling:
:

	Ovs	Mdns	Runs	Wkts	Ave
T.W.Wall	75	13	189	8	23.62
D.D.J.Blackie	210	52	444	14	31.71
J.Ryder	68.5	16	188	5	37.60
H.L.Hendry	165	51	328	8	41.00
C.V.Grimmett	398.2	95	1024	23	44.52
J.M.Gregory	41	2	142	3	47.33
P.M.Hornibrook	67	12	193	4	48.25
R.K.Oxenham	200	71	349	7	49.85
H.Ironmonger	162.3	59	306	6	51.00
A.G.Fairfax	34	4	104	2	52.00
E.L.a'Beckett	177	51	216	2	108.00
O.E.Nothling	46	5	72	0	-
C.E.Kelleway	34	9	77	0	-
A.F.Kippax	8	4	13	0	-

Individual Performances in the Tests

England Batsmen:

> 251 - W.R.Hammond at Sydney (Second Test)
> 200 - W.R.Hammond at Melbourne (Third Test)
> 177 - W.R.Hammond at Adelaide (Fourth Test)
> 169 - E.H.Hendren at Brisbane (First Test)
> 142 - J.B.Hobbs at Melbourne (Fifth Test)
> 137 - M.Leyland at Melbourne (Fifth Test)
> 135 - H.Sutcliffe at Melbourne (Third Test)
> 119 - W.R.Hammond at Adelaide (Fourth Test)

Australia Batsmen:

> 164 - A.Jackson at Adelaide (Fourth Test)
> 123 - D.G.Bradman at Melbourne (Fifth Test)
> 112 - H.L.Hendry at Sydney (Second Test)
> 112 - J.Ryder at Melbourne (Third Test)
> 112 - D.G.Bradman at Melbourne (Third Test)
> 111 - W.M.Woodfull at Sydney (Second Test)
> 107 - W.M.Woodfull at Melbourne (Third Test)
> 102 - W.M.Woodfull at Melbourne (Fifth Test)
> 100 - A.F.Kippax at Melbourne (Third Test)

England Bowlers:

> J.C.White - 8 for 126 at Adelaide (Fourth Test)
> H.Larwood - 6 for 32 at Brisbane (First Test)
> G.Geary - 5 for 35 at Sydney (Second Test)
> G.Geary - 5 for 105 at Melbourne (Fifth Test)
> J.C.White - 5 for 107 at Melbourne (Third Test)
> J.C.White - 5 for 130 at Adelaide (Fourth Test)
> J.C.White - 4 for 7 at Brisbane (First Test)
> M.W.Tate - 4 for 77 at Adelaide (Fourth Test)
> M.W.Tate - 4 for 99 at Sydney (Second Test)

Australia Bowlers:

> D.D.J.Blackie - 6 for 94 at Melbourne (Third Test)
> C.V.Grimmett - 6 for 131 at Brisbane (First Test)
> T.W.Wall - 5 for 66 at Melbourne (Fifth Test)
> C.V.Grimmett - 5 for 102 at Adelaide (Fourth Test)
> R.K.Oxenham - 4 for 67 at Adelaide (Fourth Test)
> D.D.J.Blackie - 4 for 148 at Sydney (Second Test)

1928/29 Australian Tour Averages

Batting:

	Inns	N.o.	Runs	H.S.	Ave
W.R.Hammond	18	1	1553	251	91.35
D.R.Jardine	19	1	1168	214	64.88
E.H.Hendren	17	1	1033	169	64.56
L.E.G.Ames	8	3	295	100	59.00
J.B.Hobbs	18	1	962	142	56.58
H.Sutcliffe	16	0	852	135	53.25
M.Leyland	17	3	614	137	43.85
C.P.Mead	14	3	459	106	41.72
E.Tyldesley	16	2	509	81	36.35
A.P.F.Chapman	17	1	533	145	33.31
H.Larwood	14	0	367	79	26.21
M.W.Tate	17	1	322	59	20.12
G.Geary	16	3	215	66	16.53
J.C.White	18	7	137	30	12.45
G.Duckworth	13	6	84	39	12.00
A.P.Freeman	7	3	42	17	10.50

Bowling:

	Balls	Mdns	Runs	Wkts	Ave	balls/run
J.C.White	5179	233	1471	65	22.63	3.52
G.Geary	2824	104	956	37	25.83	2.95
M.W.Tate	4148	174	1325	44	30.11	3.13
H.Larwood	2774	61	1258	40	31.45	2.20
A.P.Freeman	2433	35	1136	35	32.46	2.14

D.R.Jardine	126	2	67	2	33.50	1.88
W.R.Hammond	1600	50	661	11	60.09	2.42
M.Leyland	754	12	357	4	89.25	2.11
E.H.Hendren	120	2	57	0	-	2.10
H.Sutcliffe	32	1	18	0	-	1.77
G.Duckworth	8	0	7	0	-	1.14
C.P.Mead	8	0	11	0	-	0.72

N.B. In the Tests, six balls were bowled an over. In the other matches, eight balls were bowled an over.

The figures demonstrate that not only did Jack White take the most wickets at the best average of runs per wicket; but also that he was by far the most economical of the bowlers in terms of conceding runs/over.

APPENDIX 3
Three Studies in Greatness – From Wisden 1978

JOHN CORNISH WHITE, who died in the first week of the 1961 cricket season, having exactly completed three score years and ten, was one of the best left-arm slow bowlers of all time. From his first appearance in the Somerset side in 1909 when he was seventeen until he retired in 1937 he took over 2,350 wickets and only fourteen bowlers in cricket history have done better.

From 1921 to 1930 he played in 15 Tests for England and toured both Australia and South Africa. On the triumphant tour of 1928-29 when England beat Australia 4-1 in the Test rubber he was vice-captain to Percy Chapman and never before or afterwards did he demonstrate his prowess or endurance to such effect. England won the first Test at Brisbane, which has been a postwar bogey ground for us, by the incredible margin of 675 runs. When sunshine followed rain in the night White took four prime Australian wickets for seven runs in less than seven overs. From the fourth Test at Adelaide England eventually emerged victors by 12 runs. In boiling heat White performed with an untiring skill matched by unflagging accuracy and endurance, sending down just on 125 overs and coaxing 13 wickets out of that shirt front pitch. They cost him 256 runs but on a batsman's paradise England got home on a whisker, thanks to White.

In the last Test Chapman was ill and White led England in a match which lasted eight days and was at that time the longest Test ever played. Weary and weakened England lost but as they had won the first four it was no sort of compensation to the Australians. Monty Noble, Australia's captain for most of the first decade of this century, said of White, "One of the most tireless workers with muscle and brain that this or any other England team has ever possessed. On bad, worn and good wickets alike White was always able to call the tune and compel the batsman to dance to it. A truly capable, modest, unassuming sportsman, Jack White."
Oddly enough no one in Britain ever called him Jack. He was known in the game and by the fans either as "the Jasper" or "Farmer".

He was in fact the son of a well-to-do cricket-loving farmer, being born at Holford near Taunton on February 19, 1891. Educated at Taunton School, he came under the influence of a former cricket professional, E.J. Tyler, and he learned much of what he knew about bowling from his coach and mentor, but as Tyler said, "A coach can only do so much. Greatness of the kind J.C. White possessed comes from inside a man."

At this point I must attempt to define what made "Farmer" a world-class left arm spinner by any standards at any given period in cricket's development. He took 100 wickets or more in a season fourteen times and even modern heroes like Statham, Trueman, Don Shepherd, Laker, and Alec Bedser never accomplished that.

Where to start? Well, he obviously had the two greatest virtues of his kind – uncanny command of length and the ability to make the ball really spin. To these he added all the cunning and concentration of a nimble mind. If he got on a wicket that was "doing a bit" he pitched the ball on the leg stump of a right hand batsman and made it go fizzing across him. He used sparingly a faster ball that was invariably deadly because he never varied his approach or run up to the bowling crease. On hard pitches giving him no help he concentrated his attack on flight, varied with a slight swerve or wobble in the air and a tempting slow ball well outside the off stump to which he imparted an extra degree of real finger spin. He had an armoury to exploit every possible combination of conditions.

If the wind helped him he could make the ball dip disconcertingly and he swerved it late. If the wind was against him he could still make the ball swerve but so superb was his control he could lessen the swerve. "You must guard against making the ball do too much" he used to warn young bowlers who sought his help and advice. He was blessed with an iron constitution that helped him to prolong his career until shortly before the Second World War. He remained economical to the end and his great haul of wickets cost him fewer than nineteen runs each.

White was a regular in the Somerset side as early as 1913 and but for the First World War would probably have taken 3,000 wickets. By 1928 he was the Somerset captain and another aspect of his greatness then made itself apparent. He allowed his professional bowlers to pick the end they fancied, quite happy to operate at the other. "Farmer" of course was so good that he could take wickets from the end no one else wanted.

He was a long way from being a mug with the bat. He scored over 12,000 runs and in 1929 and 1930 completed the double of 1,000 runs and 100 wickets in a season, although he always roared with laughter at any suggestion that he was an all-rounder. "My ground fielding is shocking sometimes" he would say as justification for his mirth. It was not too bad when the ball was in the air, for he clung on to some 400 catches in his illustrious career. When England beat South Africa two-nil with three matches drawn in 1929 White was captain on three occasions. He once said to Gubby Allen "I can't think why they keep calling on me to do the job. Don't they know we've all got straw in our hair down in Somerset?"

One side who knew differently was Worcestershire. In 1919 he took 16 of their wickets for 83 runs in a single day at Bath. Two years later at Worcester he took all ten wickets in an innings for 76.

By the time cricket was started up again after the Second World War the name J.C. White had no magic for the fans, but those inside the game would never forget him. For a time he served as an England selector and his counsel was always heard at Taunton with reverence. Fond of all forms of sport, he lost an eye in a shooting accident but his life was crowned in its final year when the county which had given him a chance at the age of 17 made him its President over half a century later.

BIBLIOGRAPHY

Robertson-Glasgow, R.C. - *Crusoe on Cricket- The Writings of...*
Hendren, Patsy - *Big Cricket*
Moorhouse, Geoffrey - *Lord's*
Gibson, Alan - *The Cricket Captains of England*
Plumtree, George - *The Essential E.W.Swanton*
Swanton, E.W. - *Sort of a Cricket Person*
Frith, David - *The Golden Age of Cricket (1890-1914)*
Andrews, Bill - *The Hand That Bowled Bradman*
Robertson-Glasgow, R.C. - *46 Not Out*
Noble, M.A. - *The Fight for the Ashes 1928/29*
Thomson, A.A. - *Cricketers of my Time*
Brown, John - *Independent Witness*
McLean, Teresa - *The Men in White Coats*
Lemmon, David - *The Great Wicket-Keepers*
Lemmon, David - *Percy Chapman*
Tate, Maurice - *My Cricketing Reminiscences*
Howat, Gerald - *Walter Hammond*
Harte, Chris - *A History of Australian Cricket*
Bradman, Sir Donald - *The Art of Cricket*
Buchanan, Handaryde - *Great Cricket Matches*
Lemmon, David - *The Great All-Rounders*
Lewis, Tony - *MCC Masterclass*
Murphy, Patrick - *The Spinner's Turn*
Foot, David - *Sunshine, Sixes and Cider*
Roberts, Ron - *Sixty Years of Somerset Cricket*
Rogerson, Sidney - *Wilfred Rhodes*
Pridham, Major C.H.B. - *The Charm of Cricket (Past and Present)*
Somerset County Gazette Series
The Tauntonian 1905-1910
The Hamlyn A-Z of Cricket Records
The Times

INDEX